PERGAMON INTERNATIONAL LIBRARY
of Science, Technology, Engineering and Social Studies

The 1000-volume original paperback library in aid of education,
industrial training and the enjoyment of leisure

Publisher: Robert Maxwell, M.C.

Reporting
U.S.-European
Relations

THE PERGAMON TEXTBOOK
INSPECTION COPY SERVICE

An inspection copy of any book published in the Pergamon International Library
will gladly be sent to academic staff without obligation for their consideration for
course adoption or recommendation. Copies may be retained for a period of 60 days
from receipt and returned if not suitable. When a particular title is adopted or
recommended for adoption for class use and the recommendation results in a sale
of 12 or more copies the inspection copy may be retained with our compliments.
The Publishers will be pleased to receive suggestions for revised editions and new
titles to be published in this important international Library.

Pergamon Titles of Related Interest

Clark POLITICS AND THE MEDIA: Film and Television for
the Political Scientist and Historian

DeVolpi et al. BORN SECRET: The H-Bomb, the *Progressive* Case
and National Security

Lehman/Burke COMMUNICATION TECHNOLOGIES AND
INFORMATION FLOW

Related Journals*

HISTORY OF EUROPEAN IDEAS
INTERNATIONAL JOURNAL OF INTERCULTURAL RELATIONS
LANGUAGE & COMMUNICATION
SYSTEM
WORLD DEVELOPMENT
WORLD LANGUAGE ENGLISH

*Free specimen copies available upon request.

Reporting
U.S.-European
Relations
Four Nations, Four Newspapers

Michael Rice
with
Jonathan Carr
Henri Pierre
Jan Reifenberg
and
Pierre Salinger

(Edited by Michael Rice with James A. Cooney)

An Aspen Institute Book

PERGAMON PRESS
New York   Oxford   Toronto   Sydney   Paris   Frankfurt

Pergamon Press Offices:

U.S.A.   Pergamon Press Inc., Maxwell House, Fairview Park,
                     Elmsford, New York 10523, U.S.A.

U.K.   Pergamon Press Ltd., Headington Hill Hall,
                     Oxford OX3 0BW, England

CANADA   Pergamon Press Canada Ltd., Suite 104, 150 Consumers Road,
                     Willowdale, Ontario M2J 1P9, Canada

AUSTRALIA   Pergamon Press (Aust.) Pty. Ltd., P.O. Box 544,
                     Potts Point, NSW 2011, Australia

FRANCE   Pergamon Press SARL, 24 rue des Ecoles,
                     75240 Paris, Cedex 05, France

FEDERAL REPUBLIC Pergamon Press GmbH, Hammerweg 6
OF GERMANY   6242 Kronberg/Taunus, Federal Republic of Germany

Copyright © 1982 Aspen Institute for Humanistic Studies

Library of Congress Cataloging in Publication Data
Main entry under title:

Reporting U.S.-European relations.

   "An Aspen Institute book."
   Includes index.
      1. Foreign news. 2. Newspapers.
3. Journalism--Political aspects. 4. United
States--Foreign relations--Europe. 5. Europe--
Foreign relations--United States. I. Rice,
Michael, 1941-   . II. Cooney, James A.
PN4784.F6R4   1982   070.4′33   81-19266
ISBN 0-08-027525-7   AACR2
ISBN 0-08-027524-9 (pbk.)

Printed in the United States of America

CONTENTS

PREFACE

Imagine that you are cut off from the newspapers of your own country. Imagine that you have to rely on the leading newspaper in another country for your information on how that country and your own are getting along in their political and cultural relations. What picture of the relevant events and issues will you find? How will it differ from the picture you would find in your home country's newspapers? Does the difference arise from disparities in journalistic practice or from larger social and cultural distinctions?

These were the questions that stirred three associates of the Aspen Institute—Shepard Stone and James A. Cooney in Berlin and Michael Rice in New York—to launch the project that has produced this book.

We knew, of course, that between the highly developed Western nations and the Third World or between the democratic West and the communist East, the news media display striking differences in outlook, style, and mission. That can be expected in societies that are so different in other ways. No one would look to *Pravda* as they might look to *The Washington Post*.

But in societies that share many values and interests, such as the United States and its European allies, can we expect that the news media will behave and look essentially alike? Or will they show significant differences of their own?

In this first inquiry we aimed not for a general assessment, but for a comparative case study. This would be an initial step, potentially noteworthy in its own right, that might suggest routes for further comparisons later on.

We limited our comparative view to the four most prominent nations in the Atlantic alliance—the United States, West Germany, Britain, and France. We narrowed our choice of the news organs to be studied to those operating in the same medium and enjoying apparently similar status in their respective societies; in each of the four countries, we chose a daily newspaper acknowledged by many to be the most influential in political affairs. We further confined our study to asking how these newspapers treated the same subject over roughly the same period, namely, the currents in U.S.–European relations from Spring through Autumn of 1980. Finally, for our critical perspectives, we chose to depend principally on 18 selected journalists—most of them experienced foreign correspondents—although their views were augmented and sometimes challenged by several politicians and other observers.

We began by inviting each of four active, accomplished journalists to monitor the coverage given to U.S.–European affairs by the chosen newspaper of the country where each was based.

Jan Reifenberg, Washington correspondent for the *Frankfurter Allgemeine Zeitung* (published in Frankfurt am Main, Germany), agreed to follow *The New York Times*. Jonathan Carr, Bonn correspondent for *The Financial Times* (London), kept watch on the *Frankfurter Allgemeine Zeitung*. Henri Pierre, London correspondent for *Le Monde* (Paris), reviewed *The Times* (London). And Pierre Salinger, Paris bureau chief for ABC News (the news division of the American Broadcasting Company television network, New York), monitored *Le Monde*.

Reifenberg, Carr, Pierre, and Salinger read and collected both the news articles and the editorials on U.S.–European relations that appeared in the newspapers they were monitoring over much the same six-month period beginning in April 1980. Working from these materials, each wrote a critical essay on the coverage and comment offered to readers by the newspaper he was asked to watch.

These essays were gathered, duplicated, and sent to some 30 journalists, diplomats, and others who had accepted invitations to attend a conference on "U.S.–European Relations as Seen in the Press," held November 9 –12, 1980, at Aspen Institute Berlin. The essays served to launch the discussions that then took place on both press and political issues.

The conference participants included one or more representatives from each of three of the newspapers studied—*Frankfurter Allgemeine Zeitung*, *The Times* (London), and *Le Monde*. *The New York Times* was also invited but declined to send a representative.

The heart of this book is the set of reviews of the four chosen newspapers. To give the reader—as much as possible within the bounds of a small volume—a direct sense of the coverage and comment these newspapers provided, each reviewer frequently quotes passages that he found characteristic of the newspaper he monitored. (The quotations from *Le Monde* and the *Frankfurter Allgemeine Zeitung* appear in English translation. The original newspaper publication date for each quoted passage is given in the American abbreviated form; for example, "6/22/80" stands for June 22, 1980.) Each essay is followed by the editor's selection of the reactions and observations it prompted from the other journalists and participants at the Berlin conference.

In the introduction, the editor offers his own description of the key findings and issues that emerged from this study, particularly as they reflect on journalistic practice.

As this book goes to press, the Aspen Institute is planning a second comparative study to deal with news media treatment of U.S.–European relations to culminate again in a review conference to be held at Aspen Institute Berlin. This time, however, the news organs under study will be four national television news services, one each again from the United States, West Germany, Britain, and France, and the period of reference will be one year later (1981).

ACKNOWLEDGEMENTS

Grateful acknowledgement for financial support of the project that led to this book is owed to Aspen Institute Berlin and to the German Marshall Fund of the United States. In addition, the editor's work would not have been possible without the general support given to the Aspen Institute's activities in the area of communications and society by the John and Mary R. Markle Foundation.

Personal thanks are especially due to the authors who, despite their more than full-time journalistic obligations, conscientiously performed the extra assignment of producing these essays; to the participants in the Aspen Institute Berlin conference of November 9–12, 1980, whose comments expanded the perspectives of this study; to Shepard Stone, James Cooney, and their associates in Berlin for much work in preparing the essay typescripts as well as in organizing the conference that met under their care; to J. Robert Moskin for helping to usher these efforts into a book; and to David Kellogg of Pergamon Press for his warm encouragement and good advice.

INTRODUCTION

Michael Rice

The essays presented in this book review how four newspapers, each in a different country, reported and commented on the political relations among their four countries over a half-year's time. The value of these essays to an understanding of politics and the press rests partly in the general patterns that emerge from their separate evidence. Such patterns are the main subject of this introductory overview. But first it is worth underscoring the particular value of the stories, arguments, and interpretations that have been taken from the newspapers themselves.

On one level these quotations can be read as a six-month history of transatlantic politics—a history assembled from the daily output of four news organizations operating independently of each other in different countries but dealing with a subject that concerns them all. These samples of journalism have been selected and appraised by four foreign correspondents of different nationalities who themselves work independently of each other, each in a country not his own. Once written, their critiques were presented for further reaction by other journalists and observers, including a few from the newspapers reviewed, and the rest from other perspectives. As collected here, these various reports and responses can serve as a quick, multisided summing up of an often stormy period in the life of the Atlantic alliance.

On another level, this book can be read as a comparative case study of the way established newspapers in four countries—countries that are more like each other than they are like the rest of the world—perceive and practice journalism. This may be an unusual comparison to make. It has been more customary to compare, say, U.S. and British news media to Third World or Communist bloc news media—an exercise where the contrasts, stemming from fundamentally opposed theories of the role of the press in society, are sharper and deeper.

In *Four Theories of the Press*, Fred Siebert, Theodore Peterson, and Wilbur Schramm categorize the news media according to the roles they play as determined by the larger social systems within which they operate:

(1) "Authoritarian" media serve the state, informing the governed of what the governors think they should know and want them to support.

(2) "Soviet Communist" media are the most developed form of the authoritarian press in our own time.

(3) "Libertarian" media, by contrast, are those outlets of expressions that are protected by basic law and custom from state interference and are under no obligation to publish anything but their own views, since a system that permits such media entrusts the individual with sorting out the truth from many competing voices. With the growth of certain news institutions to commanding size and influence, the libertarian ideal in its pure form has been left to news and opinion organs that tend to reach only fringes of the public.

(4) The mass media, including metropolitan newspapers and network broadcasters, have come to observe the "social responsibility" theory of the press. Precisely because of their extensive reach and their control of communications resources not readily available to anyone who might wish to publish or air an opposing view, these large-scale media are expected by the public or even required by the government (as in the case of U.S. broadcasters) to meet "an obligation to be socially responsible"—which is "to see that all sides are fairly presented and that the public has enough information to decide."*

All four newspapers treated in this book can be regarded as examples of news media that try to act with "social responsibility," that is, to represent some views other than their own so that the reader will be exposed to a range of contending interests. For these newspapers, this role is self-imposed and self-disciplined, although it is reinforced by what their public expects—as registered, from day to day, by what people purchase. It is also reinforced by a widely shared philosophical sense of what constitutes proper behavior for a major newspaper in a modern democracy.

This means that the differences revealed among *The New York Times*, the *Frankfurter Allgemeine Zeitung* (FAZ), *The Times* (London), and *Le Monde* do not amount to different visions of the role they as newspapers should play in the functioning of their societies. They have all come to believe in and to defend if necessary their proper independence from government, even when their editorial opinion favors the party or leaders in power. They all make efforts to offer readers a diversity of views on major, continuing issues in dispute. The comparisons to be drawn, therefore, are not at this fundamental level but at the level of journalistic

*Fred S. Siebert, Theodore Peterson, and Wilbur Schramm, *Four Theories of the Press* (Urbana: University of Illinois Press, 1956) pp. 2–6.

style, varieties of bias, standard practices, emphases in subject matter, target readership, social influence, and particular problems.

Such distinctions are important to practicing journalists, to politicians and other leaders who depend upon the news media to reach the people whose interests they would represent, and to students of the role of journalism in the life of a democracy. Some help to characterize a recognizably national style of journalism, while others, within a given style, define the identity of a particular newspaper. These are marks that not only show how newspapers differ but also, given *these* four newspapers, go far toward describing what makes a newspaper great.

Fact and Opinion

No contrast of newspaper style is more apparent, or leads to more energetic debate, than the different treatment of the journalist's own opinion. Both U.S. and European journalists who took part in this study found this to be the distinguishing difference between the "Anglo-American" and the "Continental" conventions of news reporting.

American and British newspapers take great pains (the U.S. more than the British) to divorce fact from opinion—and to make sure the *reader* knows that the *newspaper* knows when it is presenting the one, and when the other. The world of fact—that is, of observed events, demonstrable trends, quoted statements, and the other classic ingredients of what goes by the name of "objective" reporting—is the province of the "news" columns. Anything that moves beyond such description to a judgment of merits, a recommendation for action, or even a speculative interpretation is somehow set apart and labeled. It may be put on the editorial page, signifying that it is the view of those who control the newspaper overall. It may be put on the "op-ed" page, that is, the page opposite the editorial page, indicating that it is the view of the writer. It may even appear on what is otherwise a news page except that it will then be given a tag, such as "News Analysis." In reality, of course, judgmental observations find their way into news stories, just as some editorials or op-ed columns are more statements of facts than anything else. But generally what "Anglo-American" newspapers *strive* to do, however blurred the lines might become in individual cases, is to separate fact from opinion distinctly.

By contrast, Continental newspapers expect their reporters to pass judgment on what they see, hear, and write about. In this tradition, a news story is not about the course of events, but about how the reporter *assesses* the course of events. A correspondent who holds back from suggesting to the reader how to understand the merits of a public issue or an official action falls short of doing his or her whole job. For an

American reader, it would be as if the regular columns by Flora Lewis or Anthony Lewis, which appear on the op-ed page of *The New York Times,* were instead to appear as the lead news articles on page one.

This different expectation of what a news story should or should not contain can account for much of the criticism voiced by those who turn to newspapers outside their home tradition. When Henri Pierre, correspondent for *Le Monde,* samples *The Times* (London), he finds it "boring" because its stories are "colorless" and "impersonal." On the other hand, for Murray Seeger, Brussels-based correspondent for *The Los Angeles Times,* the problem with Continental news reporters in writing, say, about an official's statements is that they dwell so much on what *they* think the official meant that the reader is hard pressed to figure out what *he* actually said. In France, as Pierre Salinger explains in his essay on *Le Monde,* "Journalists are encouraged to mix information and opinion, and those who do not have a point of view are often considered dull and unreadable." He adds, however, that "Reporters for *Le Monde* have a tendency to moralize—which is exasperating for a foreign reader."

The obvious lesson for the cosmopolitan reader is to get what one can from a foreign newspaper in the light of the tradition in which it is published. The Anglo-American can look to Continental newspapers as supplements, in effect, to the editorial and opinion pages of U.S. and British papers, while the Continental reader might find in U.S. and British news pages the essential facts that are not so plainly available at home.

Bias

Finding bias is a favorite detective sport not only for outside critics of the press, but for journalists as well. In a study of newspapers in different countries, the question of bias naturally divides into two: Is there a nationalistic bias to a newspaper's treatment of foreign affairs? And is there a political bias to its treatment of contending parties and leaders within the domestic arena?

Of the four newspapers reviewed, *Le Monde* leads in presumed degree of nationalistic bias. Salinger traces this trait back to General Charles de Gaulle's role in the founding of *Le Monde.* While the original intention was that *Le Monde* "would unofficially reflect French foreign policy," what it has reflected in more recent years is "a Gaullien view of the universe, in which France is at the very center."

If other Europeans, the British, and Americans suspect that the French are generally condescending to other cultures, *Le Monde*'s particular version of this sin of pride is said to be its hostility to the United States and to West Germany.

According to Salinger, "An American reader is struck by the constant and subtle anti-Americanism that one finds in the pages of *Le Monde.* . . . There is the constant view of the Americans as naive children, interested only in money and power, and engaged in a worldwide battle to impose their hegemony on the culture and languages of other countries, notably France."

Jan Reifenberg, speaking from a German perspective, said that *Le Monde,* while "happy about the developing special relationship between France and Germany," reveals its distrust of Germany's motives. "*Le Monde* always seems to warn," he said, "that 'You have to watch those fellows.' "

Le Monde's own Henri Pierre denied that the newspaper for which he writes still exhibits an anti-German bias, but he did admit to "its mistrust, its sheer ignorance of American culture—this reflects a general phenomenon in France, a form of isolationism."

In regard to its view of Germany, *The New York Times* is subject to similar criticism. Reifenberg thinks its Bonn correspondents have been excessively critical of the German scene, particularly because of their "constant, nagging doubt as to whether today's Germans have really overcome a sordid past."

Such charges are offset by the argument from Peter Galliner of the International Press Institute that German officials are too sensitive to press criticism. Any criticism of Germany's politics, he says, "leads to an outburst in the Federal Republic."

Is *The New York Times* guilty of unwarranted anti-German sentiments? Is *Le Monde*? Or are the Germans who read these newspapers overreacting? The citations and arguments that appear later in this book may help one to reach a verdict.

Reifenberg also faults *The New York Times* more generally for "parochialism." This is explained as an apparent reluctance on the part of the editors to admit that the United States can no longer claim the dominance it enjoyed in the immediate postwar years. "Europe is either taken for granted or slapped on the hand for not behaving better," he says. "It hasn't penetrated the minds that oversee *The New York Times* that the Europe of today is not the Europe of twenty years ago; they still display a patronizing attitude."

As quoted here out of context, Reifenberg's criticism of *The New York Times* stands out as sharp, even angry. That makes reading his entire critique all the more interesting because as he cites individual articles and columns for being exceptionally balanced and sensitive to contemporary European concerns, he finds so many—by James Reston, Flora Lewis, James Goldsborough, and others—that the basis for his charge of parochialism seems elusive. Perhaps it is not what *The New York Times* does publish, but what it does not publish that is the cause for his criticism. Reifenberg takes special count of how many articles related to Europe appear on the *front* page, and how many editorials related to Europe receive *top* placement. That he finds too few of both suggests that what he objects to is not so much that *The New York Times* lacks fair and intelligent comment about Europe as that it fails to feature such comment prominently enough.

It is conceivable that this kind of dissatisfaction—like the exasperation an American reader may feel upon finding what appears to be inappropriate moralizing in *Le Monde*—stems partly from the divergent expectation one takes from home to the reading of a newspaper abroad. Writing for readers in Germany, Reifenberg can take advantage of what Melvin Lasky of *Encounter* calls their "national fetish for *long* pieces—the writers have room to move around in." The lesser tolerance that readers in other countries show for lengthiness leads even a newspaper of record like *The New York Times* to shorter pieces written to standard limits. The result may appear to give short shrift to some subjects, but whether the attention paid is indeed disproportionately meager within the newspaper's own limits depends as much on the competing subjects and how they are treated.

Thus has Max Frankel, editor of the editorial page of *The New York Times,* replied to the Reifenberg critique, somewhat tartly: "Reifenberg has every right to wish for more than one 'European' editorial a week or to deplore our preoccupation with our election and other matters. A truly perceptive critic, however, would at least have raised the question, 'compared to what?' Did we write too much on subways, or our political conventions, or our domestic economy?"

Both the *Frankfurter Allgemeine Zeitung* (FAZ) and *The Times* (London) seem to avoid arousing charges of nationalistic bias, but the role each plays in its domestic political scene is another matter. The FAZ is said by some to be in opposition to the Social Democrat-led government in Germany. Indeed, Mel Lasky says that this is partly what has made the FAZ a great newspaper: "It has had an unparalleled run—ten, fifteen years—in opposition to the government: that's always the best position for a newspaper."

Günther Gillessen, an editorial writer of the FAZ, denies that it is an opposition newspaper and maintains that it considers its positions issue by issue. On one continuing issue, however, Jonathan Carr finds that the FAZ is consistently critical of the Social Democrats (SPD) generally, and of Helmut Schmidt in particular instances. That is the issue of how to strike the balance between making pro-Soviet moves to gain the rewards of détente and strengthening German-American ties to ensure the security of Western Europe. The FAZ, according to Carr, repeatedly expresses the fear that the SPD will lead Germany toward neutralism. It was in this context that the FAZ and Chancellor Schmidt furnished the most dramatic incident to occur during this period of study between one of these four newspapers and a head of government. As explained later on in detail, FAZ's coverage of a speech delivered by Schmidt in the course of his election campaign, a speech inviting talks with the Soviets on controlling arms in Europe before NATO's intermediate-range nuclear missiles were deployed in Germany, provoked a rebuke to the FAZ by telegram from Schmidt himself in which the chancellor accused the newspaper not only of misrepresenting his position but, in so doing, of possibly misleading foreign governments in their interpretation of Germany's policy. Given so angry a reaction (and one so rare in that a head of government would take it upon himself to chastise publicly one particular newspaper), the FAZ may deny that it acts in opposition, but, so long as the Social Democrats are the ruling party, it will certainly *not* have to face charges of being *pro*-government.

The flap between Schmidt and FAZ also gave evidence, as described in Jonathan Carr's account, of how national leaders and officials sometimes communicate with each other *through* newspapers, particularly when other messages have gone awry or when it becomes important to set the record straight for onlookers as well. When the chancellor was further annoyed in the same controversy by a letter he received from President Carter—a letter that seemed to parrot the substance of the FAZ's coverage of Schmidt's thinking—he chose to vent his anger by giving an interview to the Bonn correspondent of *The Washington Post.* Similarly, when the Carter administration thought to make amends, one avenue used was an interview given to an FAZ correspondent. Although that interview was "off the record," it was plain from the contextual detail of the FAZ report that the source was National Security Adviser Brzezinski, who excused Carter's letter to Schmidt by blaming the press. Thus was a high-level international spat stirred up in the press, then settled in the press—with the press, conveniently enough, blamed by both sides for creating the dispute. In this case, using and knocking the press might be seen as the way in which both German and U.S. policy makers were able to sidetrack hard feelings as they tried to give and demand reassurance that they were still mutually committed to the same course.

The Times (London) provokes observations of bias less in terms of party politics than of class. Peregrine Worsthorne of the *Sunday Telegraph* called *The Times,* "the house organ of the political class," meaning those actively engaged in governing the country. While praising *The Times* on several counts (not least of which was the comment that its obituaries are "little bits of literature"), Worsthorne also predicted great trouble for

Times editors and correspondents in understanding and covering the ascendancy to power of conservatives in the United States under President Reagan: "Every *Times* reporter and the whole *Times* establishment are Democratic Party sympathizers. How will they manage now?"

If *The Times* has tended to favor the Democrats in its coverage of U.S. politics, that is not necessarily to be read as an indication of its position in Britain's own domestic politics. Salinger's diagnosis of *Le Monde*'s "leftist tendencies"—that they "seem to manifest themselves in almost exact proportions to the number of kilometers from Paris of the country whose problems are being treated by a *Le Monde* journalist"—makes one wonder whether *The Times'* liberal sympathies have also been a function of distance.

In regard to U.S.–European relations, Henri Pierre concludes "that *The Times'* views . . . were on the whole in line with the British Government's position." Indeed, as a foreign observer, he finds this a distinct virtue: "*The Times* affords a precious supplementary value to the foreign reader. It gives him an articulate and uninhibited view of the U.K. position regarding transatlantic problems." That *The Times* may see itself, more often than not, as a voice of British policy was implicity illustrated in an editorial (4/24/80) in which it seemed impelled to explain why it was departing in some degree from the policy of supporting the alliance by supporting the United States. "Newspapers," said *The Times*, "have a somewhat different duty and have to try and see and state the truth." A newspaper accustomed to being critical of official policy would not have to point out in a particular instance that a newspaper's duty is different from a government's.

The question of *Le Monde*'s domestic bias is bound for a new chapter with the election of François Mitterrand as president. The founding intention ascribed to de Gaulle that *Le Monde* should be the voice of official French policy toward the outside world did not prevent it from becoming repeatedly critical of de Gaulle's political heir, Giscard d'Estaing, during his latter years as president. Will *Le Monde* support Mitterrand as a champion of its own views, or will it behave like newspapers that tend over time to become critical of whoever is in power?

The New York Times drew no criticism for bias in dealing with domestic politics. Perhaps its editorial leanings are simply well enough understood to reflect the political liberalism of its home city and state. Perhaps its systematic efforts to offer a diversity of political viewpoints, particularly by means of its "op-ed" page, satisfy reasonable expectations of fairness. Perhaps most journalists involved in this study tend to share its political outlook and therefore would not think to question it.

Reporting Official Views

An aspect of newspaper practice that may reflect bias—a bias in favor of an incumbent administration or ruling party—but may stem inadvertently from the circumstances, is the reporting of views held by government leaders. On the one hand, one of the elementary expectations of any reader is that a major newspaper will describe what those who are governing the country are thinking and doing. On the other hand, the need to report official views, the assumption by government spokesmen that a newspaper cannot decline to do so, and the unwritten but observed "rules of the game" for such reporting, can add up to a persistent advantage for the office holders—an advantage that makes what the government says and what the newspaper says appear to be the same.

Pierre Salinger pointed out, indisputably enough, that a newspaper can hardly be faulted for being an accurate reporter of the government's position. But Charles Douglas-Home, Foreign Editor of *The Times*, said that there was more to the matter, that "if you regularly read a leading newspaper, you will, in some elusive way, gather a sense of the national policy positions in that country." This comes, he felt, not because a newspaper necessarily follows the government line, but because it observes the prevailing priorities. Besides, in his view, most newspapers reflect their principal sources—which are usually within the government of their own countries. "Seldom," he said, "will they [the newspapers] diverge *fundamentally* from the national drift."

The reporter's reliance on sources can itself become a code, sometimes misleading, for the reader who is trying to track the tactics of a key leader. A member of the German Foreign Office, undoubtedly prompted by an instance he has not forgotten, spoke of the problems in foreign relations that can arise if a journalist who is thought to be close to the chancellor criticizes U.S. policy: it leads people to think that the chancellor himself is the source of the criticism.

The journalist who enjoys such a "special channel" runs the risk among professional colleagues that a diligence in developing and using a top-level source in government will be seen as an excessive willingness to be used as a mouthpiece for that source, even though the information itself, precisely because it can be counted on to represent a particular policy maker's view, is valuable and perhaps otherwise unavailable. Another German official, recalling years of service in NATO, admitted to relying then more on the U.S. press than on formal channels to learn the positions of the U.S. government. "Every once in a while," he said, "you could feel it was straight from the horse's mouth."

In reading *The New York Times*, Jan Reifenberg found he could follow the sometimes contradictory currents of foreign policy in the Carter administration by looking to particular correspondents. While Bernard Gwertzman "usually reflected the prevailing attitudes at the Department of State, especially its planning staff, and also the thinking of the Secretary of State," Richard Burt "could generally be counted on to reflect the attitudes of Dr. Zbigniew Brzezinski, President Carter's national security advisor." (For this reason, perhaps, few reporters seemed surprised when Burt subsequently found a place in the Reagan administration as an assistant secretary of state.)

Some months after the period covered in this study, a column by William Safire in *The New York Times* (5/18/81) illustrated how elaborate the practice can become of reading correspondents as proxies for different officials. First he quotes one of his own colleagues; then he speculates on the source; finally he offers a different interpretation based on his own unidentified source:

> "There is reason for saying," wrote James Reston of The New York Times last week, "that President Reagan is not amused by Mr. Begin's first reaction to the new Washington Administration's policies in the Middle East. . . ."
>
> My colleague is too experienced and trustworthy a reporter to assess the President's innermost thoughts without a well-placed source. His "reason for saying," I presume, can only be that such a reading of the President's mind was given him on deep background by a high official.
>
> "Sounds like the old vicar [i.e. Secretary of State Alexander Haig]," I was told on shallower background by a different source, who may be in a better position to understand Mr. Reagan's thinking. My insider leads me to believe that. . . .

Among the more interesting aspects of this exercise in opposing sources is that Safire did not *ask* his colleague Reston whom he had relied on for his characterization of the president's views. That he did not—assuming that Reston and Safire are otherwise on at least speaking terms—might be explained by the possibility that had he actually been told the source, he would not have been able to report it without violating the rule of nonattribution by which correspondents get information "on background" from official sources. So in this case Safire gets around the rule without overtly breaking it by guessing, or at least appearing to guess ("I presume"), that Reston's source was Haig, not someone speaking directly for the president. Thereupon, based on his own "insider," he offers a substitute depiction of the president's attitude. Having done that, however, he admits to the possibility of having presumed too much in the first place:

> The source seeking to project an ominous Presidential impatience with Israel may not have been the Secretary of State, but that knock-your-ally line is indicative of the kind of wishi-washiness now emanating from the State Department.

Pity the foreign (or domestic) observer who has to rely on this sort of exegesis for a sense of what U.S. policy is.

For all its problems, however, trusting newspapers to tell what officials may think but are not saying in public is apparently too fascinating and useful a habit to give up. Günter Gillessen of FAZ put it this way: "No matter whether a bit of good information is packed into an editorial or reported as news, even if its source is not identified, you can almost smell whether or not it is authentic or trustworthy. You realize that you are very near to the source by the details, by the knowledge, by the argument."

If correspondents all of a sudden refused to report officials' views except when they could attribute them by name, they would avoid the risk of being used and compromised by the implicit bargain they make in getting newsworthy information for the price of disguising the identity of their sources. But in averting that risk, those who have managed to cultivate "special channels" would have to give up their competitive advantage over other reporters who must depend on handouts and open briefings—something they are hardly likely to do on their own initiative. The process of policy making might itself suffer from new rigidities if officials lost the ability to see new or contrary ideas tested in a public forum before having to put their own names to them.

In any case, the game is so well established and understood among the players, both journalists and politicians, that any reporter who defies it does not undo it but is simply dropped out of it. So long as that is the working reality, it presents a greater challenge to newspapers than to governments—a challenge summed up by Jan Reifenberg in his essay: "Despite its professed independence and objectivity, *The New York Times* reflects . . . official thinking in Washington so closely as to raise a fundamental question: To what degree must a newspaper maintain a healthy distance from government?"

Emphasis: Foreign Versus Domestic

The issue of proper emphasis as between foreign and domestic news has been touched on in connection with Jan Reifenberg's criticism of *The*

New York Times for granting, in his judgment, less coverage than is deserved to Western Europe and alliance affairs. As compared with the rest of the U.S. press, however, *The New York Times* might earn far better marks in this area. Joachim Fest, a publisher of FAZ, said: "Whenever I come to the United States, I find it extremely difficult to get some information about what's going on in the world outside the United States, and if I leave the East Coast, I am entirely lost. I wonder how the American administration gets its information about Europe, about the other parts of the world—I don't mean the very top people, but the average [members] of the administration. I ask myself from time to time if some of the shortcomings of American politics stem from this lack of information."

Mort Rosenblum, then editor-in-chief of the *International Herald Tribune* published in Paris, ventured what he called "the shadow concept" to explain this state of affairs. In a subsequent article for his newspaper (11/26/80), he offered it as a general phenomenon:

> Societies are concerned about those nations that cast a shadow over them rather than those over which they cast a shadow. . . .
>
> A disparate Europe does not command prime attention in the American press because it does not equal the United States in terms of political and economic weight. The United States is permanently preoccupied with the Soviet Union, its fellow superpower. . . .
>
> This shadow concept applies down the line. If the Frankfurter Allgemeine Zeitung carries numerous stories about the United States, it runs little about, say, Belgium upon which West Germany's shadow falls. Belgian papers carefully cover the United States—and also West Germany.

Even allowing for the natural logic of the shadow concept, however, Rosenblum does not assume that the result it produces is always right or adequate. In regard to coverage of Europe, he says:

> Major [U.S.] newspapers explain significant events, but they leave wide areas uncovered, ignoring information that might otherwise be considered essential if readers better understood how Europe was vital to their well-being.

If the European critique of *The New York Times* and even more of the U.S. press in general is that too little attention is paid to European affairs, this may only partly represent the judgment of the professional journalist; it may also represent the wider resentment of being, in Rosenblum's metaphor, overshadowed. The issue for U.S. editors in regard to Western Europe (or for German editors in regard to Belgium, and so forth) is whether overshadowing other societies might require knowing more, not less, about them—not out of the magnanimity that can grace being powerful, but out of the self-interest that arises from being mutually dependent, however imbalanced that mutual dependence might be.

One is reminded of the Irwin Shaw story, "The Man Who Married a French Wife." The American husband and his Parisian wife are visiting Paris where he smugly tells an old buddy who now lives there with his own French wife that he has not bothered to learn how to speak or understand French. Replies his buddy, "Take it from me: learn French."

It should be noted that Peregrine Worsthorne offered quite a different theory to explain why U.S. press coverage of Western Europe seems to have declined. Far from taking it as a sign that the United States has eclipsed Europe, he read it as evidence that U.S. influence in Europe has diminished. He said the same thing happened in Britain in regard to those parts of the world where British power had waned. "The political class," in Worsthorne's words, "will be less willing to imbibe detail if they have no *reason* to take such an interest," that is, if it does not concern people or events that they have some discretionary power to affect. That sounds like just the opposite of the shadow concept, but whatever the theory to explain it, the nature of the result is generally conceded. The U.S. press features Western Europe less than the European press features the United States. That is a problem if one believes that the United States and Europe need each other.

Readership and Influence

Comparing the social and political impact of these newspapers in their respective countries tends to center on two questions: (1) who reads them and how are they regarded by those readers? and (2) how do they fare against the competitive influence of television news?

Henri Pierre granted that *The Times* (London) is a "working tool for Britain's elite," but suggested that it should address "the average reader" instead. Charles Douglas-Home replied that it does, that its target reader is the eighteen-year-old who is about to leave school. Pierre criticized *The Times* for continually spelling out the competing considerations of an issue without coming to a conclusion. Eugene Blabey of United Press International defended *The Times* in this respect for being properly "educational."

Jan Reifenberg, too, argued that "A newspaper should be not only an opinion-maker, a chronologist of current events, but also an educator in the largest sense of this word." This is a high aim with which few defenders of the press would take issue. That it should have to be articulated at all in the company of distinguished journalists, however, disclosed some unease about how a newspaper can meet high standards and still serve the average reader, not to mention how it can survive as a business.

Douglas-Home regretted that *The Times* had not tried to change in ways that would attract and appeal to more readers. The fear was that this could be achieved only at the price of lowering standards. He himself thought that maintaining high standards and being more interesting were not necessarily incompatible, but he got little support for this view by analogy with *The New York Times,* which William Pfaff, a writer for *The New Yorker* and the *International Herald Tribune,* felt had decided "to get more popular or become more accessible, and what happened was a great trivialization." Or, as Mel Lasky put it, *The New York Times* "now goes for a million readers: its big story is the Big Apple."

By comparison, *Le Monde* and the FAZ were held up as examples of newspapers that manage to prosper while remaining serious and still striving to provide comprehensive world affairs coverage. In their cases, the excellence of their coverage and commentary was cited as the source of their influence on home ground.

The influence of *The Times* and *The New York Times* was conceded to be as great or greater in the political life of Britain and the United States, but more, it was implied, by their traditional place in the habits and customs of their up-scale readers than by consistently thorough coverage of important foreign developments.

According to Salinger, the influence of *The New York Times* in Washington is so great because it is presumed, like *The Washington Post,* to be read in the White House. (He might have said the same about *The Times* of London and 10 Downing Street.) If, say, *The Los Angeles Times* provided superior foreign affairs coverage, that would not assure it equal or greater influence. To compete by that measure, it would not only have to be immediately delivered to or published in Washington, but widely read there as well. With the dawning in the United States of national editions of major newspapers (thanks to communications satellites, which *The Wall Street Journal* has proved can feed regional printing presses for timely delivery nationwide), this dimension of competition—for the attention of policy makers and all those who deal with them—may indeed open up. In that event, would *The New York Times* or *The Washington Post* be spurred to offer more international political coverage, or might the pressure of further competition make it even harder for them to do so? Finally, the president of the United States pays no more for his daily newspaper than any other reader. For the publisher, *how many* will buy must, up to a point, speak more insistently than *who* will buy.

Meanwhile, television news seems to be running away with the prize of having the broadest influence with the general public in each of these countries. Newspaper influence, said Pierre Salinger of ABC News, is "miniscule" by comparison.

Mort Rosenblum reminded Salinger, however, that the secondary influence of these major newspapers is incalculably greater than can be demonstrated by their own circulations, and it is so precisely because the electronic news media tend to look to the print media for their cues on what to report. As he put it, speaking of journalism in the United States, "All correspondents—including those who report for television—tend to refer to *The New York Times* to validate what is or is not a story."

Rosenblum's point cuts through the usual debate in which print journalists bemoan the coming of television news broadcasting and the commanding success of its "lightning-flash journalism," the phrase attributed to Hodding Carter, press spokesman for the State Department in the Carter administration, denoting the instantaneous, but only momentary, attention that television typically, in his view, pays to events. The more likely truth is that television has not taken away readers from the sort of newspaper reporting that foreign correspondents produce. The readers of newspapers committed to intellectually serious coverage of political affairs have always been a minority of the public. It can even be argued that newspapers of this sort are more broadly influential on public opinion than ever before—not directly, of course, but through their proxies, the television news professionals who are their most avid and dependent readers, second only to government press secretaries. *The New York Times* is indeed read every morning in the White House because it is, among other things, a premonition of what will be on the nightly network news broadcasts, when millions of people across the nation will be watching. The one medium feeds the other. With rare exceptions, though abstract discourse tends to stop at the printed page, the *news* content on national television is the same as in newspapers except in degree of detail.

Problems

The discussions prompted by these essays identified two sets of problems facing newspapers that are trying to build or maintain a reliable standard of foreign affairs coverage: problems with recruiting and retaining top foreign correspondents, and problems with holding the attention of the public.

While the popular notion of a foreign correspondent may be that of a glamorous and much sought-after role, the reality is that even leading newspapers are finding it more difficult to get their best reporters to accept foreign assignments than was true in the past. For one thing, the income rewards have been eroded by the inflation of living costs abroad, which have tended to outstrip salary increases. (The fact that, according to Pierre Salinger, U.S. television networks do not have the same problem in attracting people to foreign posts only underscores the newspapers' problem: television offers much higher salaries.) For another thing, fewer correspondents are willing to uproot or be separated from their families, particularly in cases where a spouse is pursuing his or her own career.

Dennis Redmont, Rome Bureau Chief for Associated Press, points out that the cost of maintaining a newspaper or news agency correspondent abroad now ranges from $100,000 to $150,000 a year. To some extent, new communications technologies have made it possible to reduce the ranks of intermediary staff and thus partially offset other rising costs. Such cost cutting can take its toll, however, from the quality of a correspondent's work. Jan Reifenberg types his own teletype messages from Washington to the FAZ in Frankfurt in a working day that starts at 6:00 AM and goes to 9:00 PM. "Ideally," he says, "one should have time to read books, but so consuming are the technicalities of the job, you have to take it out of your own flesh to do that."

The balance a newspaper strikes between using news agency reports and its own correspondents is a question not only of cost but of editorial reputation. "In an ideal world," says Charles Douglas-Home, "you would rely on the agencies for spot news and use your own people for the broader views, but it would take a psychological revolution to overcome the ritual requirement of having your own correspondent on the hard news." This, he regrets, is the "tyranny of yesterday's events," making it harder to develop journalists who can attach to those events "the indices of longer-term change."

UPI's Eugene Blabey believes the feeling is prevalent among newspaper editors that news agency reports are their "last resort even when their own correspondent is not on top of a story or even anywhere near it."

Replying from his vantage point as a foreign correspondent, Jonathan Carr takes issue with relying on the agencies to provide all the hard news: "The minute you step away from news events in order to do background, your work suffers from your not being there yourself."

The discipline of continual hard-news reporting may be inseparable from the excellence of a correspondent as a longer-range analyst. Mort Rosenblum worries that "more and more, reporters are writing what they *don't* know—the result of an analytic style that is evolving into regular practice."

Murray Seeger is blunter: "You can't overestimate ignorance as the basis for bad reporting."

In recruiting and giving experience to new correspondents, the editors participating in this study have found two common—and trouble-some—traits. One is that most people who choose to enter the field bring along personal or ideological sympathies with the political left. This poses a constant underlying challenge to editors who want to en-sure balanced, if not impartial, reporting in their news pages. A second trait that may go hand in hand with the first is that, knowingly or not, the newcomers tend to slip from the role of reporter into that of advo-cate. These problems are discussed in the comment sections following the essays.

The other set of commonly experienced problems has to do with the public—more specifically, how to arouse newspaper readers to a strong and consistent interest in alliance relations and foreign affairs generally.

Günther Gillessen of FAZ contrasts the situation today with the situa-tion in 1945. From then through the years of reconstruction, the Ameri-cans and Germans were just discovering each other. Young Germans went to the United States to study and returned to report what they found. Most American security interests were focused on Europe. "Now," Gillessen says, "the U.S. seems so well-known to Germans that there is no reason to go there except to visit relatives—or Yellowstone Park." From the U.S. viewpoint, moreover, the prevailing interest has shifted to the overall competition with the Soviet Union, extending well beyond Europe to the Middle East and other areas. The question, as Gillessen puts it, is "how to create a new sense of mutual curiosity while avoiding a sense of *deja vu.*"

Pierre Salinger attributes the American public's lesser interest in Europe to the political facts of the case. Having to deal for the most part bilaterally with each European country, the United States finds it rel-atively pointless to try to view or learn about Europe as a whole. "This won't change," he says, "until Europe itself is a valid, coherent united force, with which the U.S. will then have to reckon more seriously."

Agreeing, Jonathan Carr allows that from Washington the disarrayed Europeans must appear to be "a pathetic little bunch." But he finds somewhat the same problem with the United States. "Is it too much," he asks, "that on both sides we know our own minds and then speak to each other at the appropriate times and levels?" He cites the confusion of signals that came from the Vance and the Brzezinski camps in the Carter administration—a confusion hardly improved upon by the conflicting statements of Defense Secretary Casper Weinberger and Secretary of State Alexander Haig that marked the beginning of the Reagan administration.

The thesis underlying this view is that newspapers will not be able to foster a climate of interest and understanding between people in the United States and in Europe until communications are improved at top government levels. "It was an absurd spectacle," in Carr's view, "that the Western countries could not talk with each other in the face of a string of crises. We need a new forum or other mechanisms that will bypass the old ones—first among France, Germany, and Britain to formulate a strong European view, and then between them and the U.S."

Douglas-Home also thinks such a mechanism is needed if Americans are to see Europe as an entity. " 'NATO' has been phenomenally useful," he says, "because the name immediately plugs people into something familiar to them. 'European-American relations' is a subject too nebulous to absorb. A reading public needs a framework for understanding these relations comparable, say, to the benchmark occasions in domestic politics—the Queen's Speech in Britain or the President's State of the Union in the U.S., for example. 'EEC,' even to the British, is too nebulous: its benchmarks have not yet been established in public expectations. To remedy that, there must be recurrent occasions—like elections—when Europe can command both press and public attention. As for the wider alliance, it will take something on the order of a summit meeting to bring it home."

If these comments reveal a concern that Americans tend to ignore Europe, the European view of the United States is thought to be shortsighted. "The main task for the European correspondent in the U.S.," Reifenberg aruges, "is to detach himself from day-to-day events and to present the more complex picture, but too many of them stay in Washington and never get out. 48% of the U.S. electorate did *not* vote in the 1980 Presidential election: who covers *them?* With an exclusive focus on Washington, Europe risks—with a change in Administration—both exaggerated and distorted expectations of what the change means."

William Pfaff saw a tendency, in the wake of national elections, to see the strains in relations, as reflected in the press, in terms of personalities—Carter and Schmidt as opposed to Reagan and Schmidt, and so forth. The problem, he felt, stems rather from the loss of a foreign policy consensus and the rise of unresolved competing views in both the United States and Europe. The "containment" strategy for dealing with the Soviet Union, to the extent it succeeded, led logically to détente, but with the USSR's unexpected initiatives in Africa, the Mideast, and elsewhere in recent years, and with the emergence of the oil issue, two notions of what the West should do have come into conflict: to pursue arms controls (for which Europe is more eager than the United States), and to strengthen the West in its rivalry, military and otherwise, with the Soviet Union (with which the United States is increasingly preoccupied). A mirror to these conflicting notions is the split over how to deal with the Third World—to negotiate around mutual resource dependencies, or to try to intimidate developing countries into good behavior.

In this light, the news of U.S. relations with Europe was not expected to be much different under President Reagan than it was under President Carter. Blabey predicted that Reagan would not focus on Europe (as compared with acting in the Middle East or discouraging the competition of Japanese goods in the American market) because no great domestic benefit could come of it. Pfaff believed that Europe would be interesting to the United States only as an adjunct to America's relations with the Soviet Union.

The projection of how these newspapers will treat U.S.–European relations in the future thus follows from the relative importance the governments of these countries attach to each other's role in the larger realm of superpower rivalry. The logic unfolds like this: (1) government leaders set the priority; (2) their priority gives the public reason to be interested; and (3) the interest thus stimulated gives newspapers the reason to provide coverage. A newspaper—in its editorials and choice of stories—can question that priority and try to redress an imbalance it may perceive in the official outlook, but it still cannot avoid reflecting the government's lead. That helps to explain why the examinations of individual newspapers that appear in this book so frequently go beyond the aspects of journalistic practice to the very substance of the politics at issue between the United States and its European allies. If coverage follows politics, then politics helps to determine what that coverage will be like.

Implications

For those who are awed by what they believe to be the power of the press, the picture of newspaper influence that emerges from these comments by working journalists will seem surprisingly modest. At one point in the discussions, Shepard Stone of Aspen Institute Berlin had to caution against "talking ourselves into thinking that newspapers are unimportant." Undoubtedly, the comparison with television's splashier impact contributed to this shared sense of a newspaper's limited sway with public opinion. But the more significant perceived limitation— because it was assumed to apply to all news media—was that of the agenda imposed by those in governing positions in the society. This sense of limited influence vis-à-vis the political leadership is in sharp contrast to the sort of initiative role in agenda setting that has commonly been attributed to the media in recent years. While the news media's cumulative impact can elevate some issues to special prominence, from the vantage point of a single newspaper, to stir the public's and policy makers' attention to an issue they would otherwise ignore seems neither easy nor often realized. It is the top official who can determine more decisively what is or is not a newsworthy issue.

Russell Baker, in his customary fashion, points to this phenomenon in his *New York Times* column of 6/24/81, where he marvels that "sometimes whole countries seem to go away—":

> Look at El Salvador. More precisely, just try to find El Salvador to look at. How long has it been since it suddenly popped out of the oceans to become the new absolutely vital war zone where Communism absolutely had to be stopped? . . .
> So far as I can make out, El Salvador has disappeared. It dropped back under the oceans after the Reagan people advised the news industry to revise its geography book. . . .
> I am told that the Reagan people can make El Salvador come back whenever they are ready for it, but at the moment it is inconvenient.
> Inconvenience is one of the main reasons countries go away.

That news coverage tends to adhere to official priorities is hard to fault at times when there is no well-founded disagreement that those priorities are the right ones. But the tendency raises suspicions that worry journalists themselves—suspicions that it betrays a newspaper's insufficient enterprise, that it expresses an ingrained reflex to support the established order, or that it reveals the overwhelming dominance that has been achieved by the government's own publicity machines. The price a newspaper pays for closeness to official power is that its own power becomes a parody.

How to buck the official view of what constitutes news—or, in some cases, whether or not to try to—is an unresolved question for even leading newspapers. The entourage of journalists who trail after visiting heads of state (even the president of Mexico brought along 120 on his trip to Germany) is a spectacle to make anyone wonder about the stories *not* covered owing to such a herdlike concentration of resources. The remedy, to the editor or correspondent who pursues less conspicuous subjects, can seem thankless and unprofitable: it means defying hard-news instincts and pushing forward on something else that may appear soft or irrelevant to others. The journalists who took part in this study all agreed on the need for such counterinitiatives, but they agreed as well on the difficulty of sustaining them.

Another general implication to come out of this exercise is that newspapers are being measured, however tentatively, against a new ideal, a cosmopolitan ideal. The concerns raised over any newspaper's persistent expression of a narrow nationalism imply that the most desirable newspaper would be one that could be read with equal confidence by Americans, Germans, the French, the British—indeed by anyone from outside the newspaper's country of origin. Given that measure, a great newspaper would necessarily be an international newspaper not just in what it chooses to cover, but in how it is written.

Foreign correspondents, understandably, might come to this ideal more naturally than publishers and editors whose first eye is on their own home market of readers. But if impartiality in covering domestic politics long ago became the stance of newspapers aspiring to a large general circulation, then this newer ideal represents an extension of the same impartiality to the international plane. Quite apart from the political or philosophical values that contribute to such an ideal, it may also be encouraged by the growth of multinational newspaper holdings. A newspaper institution may come to regard itself as not only above internal party politics, but above national interests as well. But if it should gain respect abroad by this course, the question is whether it would still hold and satisfy its home readers.

In this connection, it should be emphasized that *The New York Times, The Times, Le Monde,* and the *Frankfurter Allgemeine Zeitung* were all found to approximate this ideal. They drew criticism for gaps in coverage or for certain biases, but it had to be conceded that no reader would be terribly misled or left grossly uninformed if forced to rely on just one of these newspapers for reports on the thinking of policy makers in all four countries. Comparing these newspapers, one can see, of course, that Europeans view the world somewhat differently from Americans, and the Europeans themselves are rarely united in a single view, but at the same time one can find out from each newspaper what those contrasting views *are.*

The key question is not whether these newspapers define international relations identically, but whether they give their readers a fair rendering of foreign perceptions and policies that may be in dispute with their own country's. This, as a reading of the essays in this book will show, they generally do provide. One is struck, in fact, by the parallels evident in the editorial and background analyses that were selected, without advance cross-reference, from these separate newspapers. It might have been more exciting to find great disparities or distortions and to demonstrate that the conduct of alliance relations had materially suffered as a result, but, for the sake of future relations between the United States and Europe, it is comforting, even encouraging, that such were not the findings.

These and other newspapers could still greatly improve, however, their effectiveness in providing a diversity of opinion to their readers. The formats to accomplish this at the domestic level seem well established. Publishing letters to the editor, running guest columns, and purposely hiring or featuring columnists who tend to oppose a newspaper's own editorial slant are all effective ways of ensuring a breadth of views on national and local politics within the pages of the same paper. But these techniques are less frequently used at the level of international politics. Instead, the characterization of a foreign government's position is typically provided by a newspaper's own correspondent or columnist. The foreign perspective is allowed to speak for itself only when quoted in the context of the correspondent's own analysis. Most readers welcome this as an efficient alternative to trying on one's own to read between the lines of foreign pronouncements. Simply as a safeguard against inadvertent misrepresentation, however, each of these newspapers should consider making the guest column by a writer, politician, or correspondent of another country a more frequent feature of its opinion pages. Presenting a foreign viewpoint that tells "how it looks to us" is a service that can help readers, too, to develop the cosmopolitan understanding that is increasingly an ideal of journalists themselves.

Table I.1. Circulation, Staff, Journalists, and Foreign Correspondents.

	Circulation	Staff	Journalists	Foreign Correspondents
Frankfurter Allgemeine Zeitung	330,000	800	150	35
Le Monde	500-550,000	1,300	200	40 [a]
The New York Times	900,000 daily 1,460,000 Sunday	5,000	approx. 850 [b]	35
The Times	300,000	3,750 [c]	270 [d]	17 [e]

a 20 are full-time.
b The *NYT* estimates the number of journalists at 15-20 percent of the staff.
c Includes all staff for *The Times* Newspaper Group.
d Includes just journalists for *The Times* newspaper.
e Includes only the foreign correspondents exclusive to *The Times*.

Source of Information: The International Press Institute (London: May 1981).

chapter one

FRANKFURTER ALLGEMEINE ZEITUNG:
The World At Length

*Jonathan Carr**

Background

The *Frankfurter Allgemeine Zeitung* (FAZ) is a newspaper of high ser-
iousness—accurate in its reporting, thorough in its analysis, and
jealous of its independence. Very few people in West Germany involved
in political or business decision making can manage without it. The
current daily circulation (at end 1980) is more than 330,000 copies
(226,000 by subscription), and the total readership is estimated at well
over one million.

This does not imply that the FAZ is an easy read. The paper repays
diligent study but it does not invite a quick browse. It can be bland, even
dull. But when it feels deeply on an issue (such as the East-West missiles
imbalance addressed in the course of this study), then it can let fly with
startling trenchancy. Its views are often described as conservative,
which is fair so long as that does not imply automatic attachment to the
views of the right-wing political parties.

The FAZ was founded in 1949, the year in which the Soviet blockade
of Berlin ended in failure and the Federal Republic of Germany (West)
and the German Democratic Republic (East) were born. This timing
helps explain the rubric, "Zeitung für Deutschland" (Newspaper for

---

*Bonn Correspondent, *Financial Times* (London)

Germany), which the FAZ always carries on its title page. The FAZ is clearly trying to reach and speak for all Germans including those in the communist East who cannot express their opinions freely.

In some ways the FAZ can be seen as a successor to the old *Frankfurter Zeitung*, which struggled to keep an independent voice until it was stifled by the Nazis in 1943. Part of the editorial staff of that newspaper later joined the FAZ. While the *Frankfurter Zeitung* concentrated on business affairs, the FAZ sought from the first to keep a broad balance among political, economic, and cultural affairs. It is not intended simply to be a paper for experts. Hence the word, "Allgemeine," meaning "general" (if not quite universal). Its "Feuilleton" pages covering art, literature, music, culture in the broadest sense, and its weekend section with high-quality pictures help justify that claim to a broad public.

The political circumstances of its birth—the aftermath of one dictatorship in the German Reich and the birth of another in the German East—help explain the fiercely independent character of the FAZ and its highly unusual editorial structure and ownership.

The paper has no chief editor. The political, economic, and cultural policy is laid down by a group of "Herausgeber," here meaning "editor-publishers." Present members of the group are Bruno Dechamps, Jürgen Eick, Fritz Ullrich Fack, Joachim Fest, and Johann Georg Reissmüller. Their names appear every day under the FAZ's title, and one or another of them often produces the main, signed editorials on the right-hand side of the same page. Policy discords among these five are said to be rare, but when they emerge, they are settled by a majority vote.

As to ownership, each of the publishers has shares in the company, Frankfurter Allgemeine Zeitung GmbH, but together these shares still amount to only a minority stake. The company that prints the FAZ also has a minority interest. The majority holding is in the keeping of a foundation called the "Fazit Stiftung," which has five independent trustees. Any proceeds from the foundation's holding in the FAZ must go to what are called projects for the general good, including donations for university research or the training of journalists and printers. If a trustee leaves, his successors must designate a replacement. Any changes in the share holdings, either within the foundation or outside, need the approval of the "Herausgeber." If objections are raised, there are provisions for neutral arbitration.

It looks rather complicated. But the FAZ insists that nowhere is a paper's independence better safeguarded. The praise for the system from other journalists in West Germany and beyond suggests that there is merit to the claim.

Assessment

In the main editorial on the first page of the *Frankfurter Allgemeine Zeitung* (FAZ) on 8/25/80, Mr. Robert Held wrote:

> Let us drop for once the complaint we usually make when considering German-American differences—namely, that the Americans are badly informed. True, during the three weeks we were in the United States, we did not find one single, substantial report about politics in Europe in any of the papers we could get hold of. But now, in this year of 1980, we must admit that on this side of the Atlantic we can no longer pretend to be sufficiently informed about America. That which starts to divide America and Europe can no longer be bridged through the work of correspondents.

Perhaps Mr. Held is right in general about European knowledge of American affairs, but he is too hard on his own newspaper. One can disagree with some FAZ editorials on U.S.–European relations. One might like to see more about such aspects of American life as business or cultural affairs. But in general the FAZ produces astonishingly thorough coverage of the American domestic scene, of ties between the United States and Europe, and of the world developments that influence them.

Those remarks sound rather like an advertisement. I will therefore try to support them with some statistics that I hope give an idea of the range and depth of FAZ coverage.

The period I am considering in this survey is the five months from April 1 to September 1, 1980. By my count, during this period the FAZ produced 446 news stoires and 209 feature-length articles or editorials on U.S. affairs, the U.S.–European relationship, and the issues particularly affecting it. I have cast my statistical net wide, including some pieces that another person doing a similar job might not consider wholly relevant. One example is a series of feature-length articles by Mr. Thomas Ross from Afghanistan. These pieces (too long and descriptive to be usefully quoted here) seemed to give a very good "feel" for the situation there—the hardship and the heroism. A reader who followed these reports closely would have had a good factual background from which to judge the international reaction to Afghanistan—the economic embargo imposed against the Soviet Union, the Moscow Olympics boycott, and the U.S.–European squabbles.

I have divided the subject matter into nine broad categories. These are listed in Table 1.1, together with a numerical breakdown into features and news stories that may help give some idea of the weight apportioned by the FAZ to each topic.

Table 1.1. Statistical Breakdown of FAZ Coverage of U.S.–European Relations:
April 1 to September 1, 1980.

Category	News Stories	Editorials, Feature-length Articles
1. Culture, Tourism, Way of Life	24	28
2. Broad Political Relations	7	7
3. Nuclear Missiles, Carter Letter, Schmidt-Moscow	62	24
4. Western Military Strategy	35	12
5. Iran, Middle East	89	22
6. Afghanistan, Economic Boycott, Olympics	117	47
7. U.S. Election Campaign	27	39
8. Economics and Finance	72	20
9. Other, including ties with South America, China, etc.	13	10
Total	446	209
Grand Total	655	

I make no apology for putting at the top of my list "cultural affairs, tourism and way of life" (the latter definitely including the life of American forces in Germany). This is probably not an area that politicians would at once select for comment. Nor perhaps would very many journalists. (I count 24 lengthy articles and 28 news items in this subject area.) Yet surely for many people this is the most important sector, covering new trends in the visual arts, jazz, rock, sport (roller skating!), clothing, the flood of Europeans taking holidays in the United States (although apparently fewer Americans are at present coming the other way), and so on. This may seem to have little political significance, and in a narrow sense that is true. But what is emerging from the Soviet Union to affect the lives of Western Europeans so constantly and so personally? Not even an ideology any more, so far as one can judge. The Europeans and the Americans are more a part of one another than they are often ready to admit. Perhaps part of European criticism of the United States is the more biting because it is, unconsciously, self-criticism. One recalls Dylan Thomas's telling remark about "Those who condemn the American way of life as they swig and guzzle their way through it."

I shall return to this point at the end of my survey. Meanwhile, of the remaining eight categories, numbers two and three are dealt with at length. This is because the subjects, and their treatment in the FAZ, seem to me to provide the best basis for a discussion of what is going wrong in transatlantic relations and what might be done about it.

- *Category Two:* European-American political relations in the broadest sense—the attitudes on both sides that condition the reaction to each new international crisis. The FAZ naturally sees these relations through the state of Bonn-Washington ties in particular.
- *Category Three:* A special problem, the Soviet lead in intermediate-range nuclear missiles and the Western response. This has been singled out from general military questions for two reasons. It underlines particularly well some of the difficulties in communication and comprehension between the United States and West German administrations. And it involves the FAZ in particular in a dispute with Chancellor Helmut Schmidt.
- *Category Four:* Western military strategy apart from the missiles issue (but excluding the American bid to rescue the hostages in Iran and the guerrilla fighting in Afghanistan, which belong more naturally in Categories Five and Six).
- *Category Five:* Iran, the U.S. and European response (including the trade embargo), and the closely linked Middle East dispute, including the efforts of the Europeans to take a separate course.
- *Category Six:* Afghanistan, the economic boycott, and the Olympics.
- *Category Seven:* The American election campaign.
- *Category Eight:* Economics and finance.
- *Category Nine:* The rest (for example, the common and divergent U.S. and European interests in South America).

Before reviewing the items in these categories, it should be acknowledged that one cannot review the FAZ's coverage of U.S.-European relations without reviewing the substance of those relations at the same time. It is, perhaps, the highest tribute to the FAZ that a reader, even a foreign reader, is hard put to find instances where the FAZ's account of political realities departs from what one knows from other sources or is willing to consider on FAZ's authority.

Let us take the biggest question first. What impression of the state of the transatlantic partnership would a reader of the FAZ have received in these five months? The answer is gloomy but does not provoke total despair. Three examples help show why.

The first is an editorial by Mr. Jan Reifenberg, the FAZ's Washington correspondent, dated 4/15/80 and headlined "What Washington Expects." It says that "the crisis in the Atlantic Alliance has not been overcome," notes that the United States was disappointed by the failure of the European Economic Community (EEC) to take a quick decision on economic sanctions against Iran, and stresses that the Americans expect firm support from their friends.

Was West Germany excluded from U.S. criticism? After all, the Bonn government had been setting the pace in Europe on Iran sanctions, as very many FAZ news stories made clear. But apparently this fact made little durable impact in America, for on 5/19/80 Mr. Günther Gillessen of the FAZ quoted a friend and adviser to the White House as saying that Bonn-Washington ties were perhaps going through their worst-ever crisis. In this editorial, Mr. Gillessen recognized that the United States had made mistakes over the double crisis of Afghanistan and Iran, but he felt that the Europeans could and should have given more support. Specifically, he suggested that the West German government should have sought more actively to reach a joint position with Washington instead of, as he put it, taking the American guarantee of protection for granted and pressing its contacts with Moscow.

On the face of it Mr. Held, in the editorial of 8/28/80 already quoted at the start of this survey, took a less pessimistic view, but his point was still worrying enough. He said that "the relations between the Federal Republic and the U.S. are at present neither especially good nor especially bad. They have become, in a dangerous way, unclear." He stressed the differences that struck a European returning home from a U.S. visit. There the Americans, largely across party lines, had awakened to the need for greater military efforts to meet the Soviet challenge. But in Europe, the Danes had just decided to reduce spending, and the media in West Germany were full of reports of high-level contacts, either existing or pending, between Bonn and the communist countries of the East. The United States, said Mr. Held, was not out for revenge but it was concerned about European attitudes, unable to decide whether these were dictated by fear or by cold reason—*Realpolitik*.

These views have not been cited to try to demonstrate divisions among the editorialists of the FAZ. While there are some differences of emphasis, all three are agreed that there have been mistakes on both sides of the Atlantic. The balance is fair. But from these three pieces two themes emerge: one involving the whole alliance; the second involving U.S. –West German ties in particular.

The first theme is that the Iran and Afghanistan crises present Western strategists (and not only them!) with problems of hideous complexity.

Everyone is agreed that the immediate Western goal in Iran was to obtain safe release of the American hostages. But how is one best to deal with a country rent by revolutionary fervor and religious fanaticism? What influence will the Iranian revolution have on other states of the region? What impact would Western military or economic pressure on Iran have on those states and, in particular, on oil supplies? How would the Soviet Union react?

Likewise, the West is agreed on the necessity of Soviet withdrawal from, and a neutral status for, Afghanistan. But if the West is not prepared to try to drive out Soviet troops by force, by what other means is it going to achieve its goal? Will military supplies to the Afghan guerrillas help? Should one boost Pakistan's military potential—or would that risk friction with India? What kind of direct embargo against the Soviet Union, if any, would encourage it to withdraw from Afghanistan? If nothing is done, will Moscow be encouraged to intervene somewhere else?

The answers to all these questions are far from self-evident. Yet many politicians and journalists (including, I fear, some from the FAZ) have talked and written as though they are. Acting on its own behalf, the United States demonstrated time and again that it was itself not clear what combination of measures would bring the desired effect. The Europeans had similar problems. Mr. Reifenberg noted American disappointment at European slowness in imposing an embargo on Iran. No doubt many Americans felt that the Europeans were simply seeking continued benefits from trade despite the hostage drama. That sounds cynical enough to be taken as true, but it is only a half-truth. The key point is that the Europeans did not want to lose such trade as was still possible with Iran through an embargo that not only seemed unlikely to lead to the release of the hostages, but might actually intensify the Iranian will to resist "Western imperialism."

What conclusion is to be drawn from this? Surely not the simplistic one that the United States is prepared to protect allies in Europe who are not themselves ready to stand by Americans when they need help elsewhere. It is rather that the United States and Europe are being faced with more complex problems than ever before, and that the existing forms of communication, consultation, and cooperation—both in and out of NATO—appear inadequate to deal with them. The problem of Iran appears to be a microcosm of more to come: the intermingling of religious, revolutionary, and nationalistic forces not readily susceptible to outside influence; the consequences of speedy industrialization in a developing land; the danger to oil supplies and to stable markets for industrialized products. As Mr. Held said in his editorial, "It is not a question of whether the European or the American form of Realpolitik is correct or not, but of achieving durable compromise between differences of interest in the face of a major threat."

The second theme to emerge from these FAZ editorials concerns U.S.–West German relations. The Germans pressed other Europeans to go along with the sanctions against Iran; they boycotted the Olympic games and promised not to take up business lost by American firms through the partial embargo imposed by President Carter on the Soviet Union. Why then were relations between Bonn and Washington not better than Mr. Gillessen and Mr. Held suggested?

Part of the answer lies in an article by Mr. Held on 9/1/80. It surveys the results of recent opinion polls about the West German view of the United States, and initially the answers are positive. Asked which country they felt to be the Federal Republic's best friend, 53 percent chose the United States, which put it in first place, followed by France with 14 percent. Asked what was more important for the future of the German people, good relations with the United States or with the Soviet Union, 63 percent chose the former and only 12 percent the latter. When the pollsters put the same question in 1954, 62 percent had chosen Washington, 10 percent Moscow.

So far so good. But the question was also asked whether the Federal Republic should now wholly support Washington in foreign policy or decide in some cases to go its own way. Here, 30 percent of those polled spoke in favor of unqualified support, 56 percent wanted a case-by-case decision. The number of those expressing unqualified support was notably lower in the ruling Social Democrat (SPD) and liberal Democrat (FDP) parties (26 percent and 21 percent, respectively) than in the opposition CDU-CSU (43 percent).

The article does not reveal whether the last question had also been posed in 1954. But it seems unlikely that at that time more than 50 percent of West Germans would have supported a case-by-case approach to support for the United States in foreign policy, or even felt it to be possible.

There is clearly room for debate about what these results imply. But to me they suggest not that West Germans have become more anti-American, or more pro-Russian, or even more neutral over the last quarter-century, but that they have become more pro-German (or perhaps more pro-European—the data are not sufficient to make this clear).

It is hard to say whether opinion polls in Britain or France would reveal a similar trend. In any case it matters less. West Germany has gradually gained a political identity and role to match its economic and military power, which is the strongest in Europe. This role has become evident at a time when U.S. influence is generally perceived to be in relative decline. That does not mean that the Federal Republic has become—or will ever become—a superpower, or that the United States has stopped being one. But it does mean that a process has been underway that was and is almost bound to mean friction between Bonn and Washington. This friction has often been personalized in public commentary as rivalry or dislike between President Carter and Chancellor Schmidt, and no doubt the special character traits of both leaders have played a role here. It seems highly likely, however, that even with another president or chancellor in office the relations between the two countries would have been neither smooth nor easy. That is not to question Bonn's place in the Western alliance. But the West Germans now know their own weight and will not automatically accept a lead from anywhere, including Washington, without careful scrutiny and, if necessary, argument.

Further, this least dispensable of alliance members also happens to be the one that stands most to gain from a continuation of the policy of détente with the communist East. This historical accident may turn out to be a blessing in disguise (a contention that is a discussion topic in itself and cannot be dealt with here). But the point is that objective factors make the Bonn-Washington relationship a peculiarly sensitive one. It needs a special effort on both sides to maintain goodwill and trust. The details carried by the FAZ on the missiles issue (Category Three) are alone enough to show that it does not always get this.

Let us start with Fritz Ullrich Fack's 5/23/80 editorial. In it Mr. Fack suggested that Mr. Schmidt's strategy toward Moscow could not truly be compared to the appeasement policy of Chamberlain and Daladier toward Hitler in 1938 except on one point: both were supposed to achieve peace! Mr. Fack then listed aspects of Mr. Schmidt's policy and developments within the SPD that gave him cause for concern, including "the sudden weakening" of Schmidt's stand on intermediate-range nuclear missiles (Russian rockets that could reach virtually any European target directly from Soviet territory and for which NATO had no exact counterpart).

Mr. Fack here referred to the decision of December 1979 under which NATO agreed to the production of intermediate-range missiles by the United States while simultaneously offering missiles control negotiations to the Russians. It would be a good three years before the West's weapons would be available for deployment in Europe. The more successful East-West negotiations were during this period, the fewer missiles the Western Europeans would have to have on their territory—in the ideal case, none at all. Thus, one part of the NATO decision on production and deployment was indivisibly linked to the other on negotiation.

The same day Mr. Fack's editorial appeared, Mr. Schmidt sent a sharply worded telegram to the FAZ and simultaneously made public the full text of his previous remarks on the subject. The chancellor strongly denied changing his position on the missiles issue and stressed that "since a lot of notice is taken of your newspaper abroad, your false statement of facts could lead to serious misjudgment of Federal Government policy and damage our country."

The FAZ briefly noted the chancellor's denial on 5/24/80, then returned to the attack three days later. It carried both a lengthy background article from its Bonn correspondent, Claus Gennrich, and a comment from Mr. Fack. The latter said, among other things, that "this paper has never in 30 years been charged with falsifying the policy of the Federal Government—still less by a Chancellor in office. We consider this charge not only to be unjustified and damaging to our honor but also to be a massive attempt to restrict journalistic criticism. That will not work with this newspaper."

At the core of the dispute was a public suggestion by Mr. Schmidt in April that "both sides (East and West), for a certain number of years, give up installation of new or additional intermediate-range missiles and use this time for negotiations." In retrospect it is not surprising that many in the West were mystified by this suggestion, and that some were suspicious. What could Herr Schmidt have meant? He referred to "both sides" although the West so far had no such missiles of its own. And he talked about "a certain number of years" whereas NATO's missiles were expected to be ready for deployment in about three years. Was the chancellor trying to slip out of the NATO commitment?

At the risk of being pilloried by both sides, I feel the FAZ's fears were understandable but groundless and Mr. Schmidt's comments were well intentioned but unclear. There are good reasons to believe that with his comments the chancellor was trying to send a signal specifically to the Soviet Union along the lines of, "For God's sake, at least stop deploying your missiles (even if you continue to produce them) so that talks with the West can get off the ground. Otherwise another round of the arms race is as certain as eggs are eggs." Put that way, of course, the onus is clearly on the Russians, and it seems that Mr. Schmidt deliberately wrapped up his proposal in circumlocutions that might help Moscow to accept without a loss of face. He could hardly admit this later—and the wisdom of the tactic, not least the circumstances in which it was made, is questionable. Mr. Schmidt spoke at an SPD gathering in Hamburg for which no advance text was available. It was hard enough for the press in Bonn to find out what he said, let alone for Moscow to realize that a signal was being sent. When Moscow did realize what was afoot, it refused.

But all that is other than saying that Mr. Schmidt was weakening a Western position that, as it happens, he had been principally responsible for creating. The chancellor was the first Western leader to draw attention publicly to the threat posed by the build-up of Soviet intermediate-range missiles. He did so in a speech in London in 1977, and his words were initially taken by the United States to mean that the West Germans wanted such missiles themselves—the opposite of the truth. Later Mr. Schmidt not only strongly argued the case (particularly in his own party) for a NATO decision of the kind that finally emerged, he also actively campaigned to see that at least some other continental European countries as well as the Federal Republic were ready to have the weapons on their territory.

It is true that a strong minority of the SPD were (and are) unhappy about the NATO stand, fearing it would simply intensify the arms race. It is also true that without both parts of that decision—negotiations as well as production—a majority of the SPD would almost certainly have been against it. It is further true that if the SPD had an absolute majority in the Bundestag (instead of an alliance with the FDP), the pressure for an alternative policy would be greater.

The question for journalists as well as diplomats is how these elements are to be balanced against the reality of the Schmidt-Genscher government, the place of the Bundeswehr in the Alliance after ten years of SPD-FDP rule, the strength of a conservative opposition that continues to collect well over 40 percent of the West German popular vote. Johann Georg Reissmüller's editorial of 4/23/80 entitled, "Where is it all leading to?" provides a typical example of the FAZ's fear with respect to the SPD in particular. Mr. Reissmüller cites the anti-American sentiment in the speeches of Willy Brandt and Rudy Arndt at a regional SPD party meeting. Mr. Brandt had said, "Don't let everyone tell us we are supposed to be more American than the Americans." He had also stated that the Federal Republic loyalties were "to Europe, to its partners, and to the United States." Reissmüller is struck that the most important ally comes last. The criticisms of the United States are bad enough, according to Mr. Reissmüller, but what he really regrets is that they have become commonplace within the SPD. The delegates loudly applauded the speeches and no one countered Brandt or Arndt. The point of the editorial is that the SPD, including Helmut Schmidt, needs to recognize what forces it is unleashing. "He who starts something has to consider the consequences. A coolness toward the U.S. can easily grow to a public anti-American feeling." And Mr. Reissmüller says that is only the beginning of the problem, because neutralism is the logical consequence of the anti-American sentiments.

Obviously it would be absurd to suggest that there are no problems,

even dangers. The difficulty is to know how much relative weight
to give them. My feeling is that overall the FAZ's commentaries present
an overly pessimistic view, particularly for a foreign reader, but that the
factual reporting by the FAZ's correspondents allow one plenty of scope
to make up one's own mind.

Whatever one may think about Mr. Schmidt's telegram to the FAZ, at
least some of his fears about the influence of the press on foreign opinion proved justified. Only about three weeks after the dispute with the
FAZ, the chancellor received what he later described as an "astonishing
and superfluous letter" from President Carter. In it Mr. Carter recalled
the terms of the NATO missiles decision and mentioned press reports
about the West German position on the issue. The president apparently
wanted to warn Mr. Schmidt not to undermine the NATO stand in talks
he was to have with the Soviet leader, Leonid Brezhnev, in Moscow on
June 30 and July 1, 1980.

Mr. Schmidt was vexed, to say the least. For one thing, he was due to
meet Mr. Carter shortly at the Venice Economic Summit conference on
June 23–24. For another he had tried to allay in advance any doubts Mr.
Carter might have had on the missiles issue by sending supplementary
details about his position to Washington. Had the president not received
these, as the reference to "press reports" suggested? Or had he received
them but taken no notice? Mr. Schmidt's anger became clear for all to see
in an interview he gave the Bonn correspondent of the *Washington Post.*
A detailed report of the interview appeared in the 6/23/80 FAZ. Pri-
vately, aides to the chancellor also made clear that they felt Mr. Carter's
National Security Affairs Adviser, Zbigniew Brzezinski, must have been
behind the affair. This was only one occasion when criticism was leveled
in Bonn at Brzezinski and at the apparent strategy of "dynamic tension" existing between the State Department and the National Security
Council.

The Bonn government saw its suspicions confirmed by, among other
things, a report from Venice dated 6/24/80, by the FAZ's Brussels correspondent, Heinz Stadlmann, one of the team covering the Western economic summit. Headlined "Everything is now fine with Schmidt for the
man from the White House," and subheaded "Does Carter often write
letters on the basis of press reports?," the article recounts an "off the
record" interview with a high U.S. official who, Mr. Stadlmann notes,
"has a lot to do with security . . . and does not have the reputation of
being particularly pro-German."

This elegant and witty report strongly conveys the impression that
Mr. Brzezinski was trying hard to clear the troubled U.S.–German
atmosphere and was partly using the FAZ to do it—whether at the direct
bidding of Mr. Carter or on his own initiative is not clear. Brzezinski

claimed that false press reports led to the letter being written, and when asked whether Mr. Carter often wrote letters on the basis of press reports, Brzezinski "smiled disarmingly and gave assurances that relations between Carter and Schmidt were fully in order."

That much was encouraging. But a detailed reading of this article reveals that while one problem might have been cleared up, other question marks remained. In particular, Brzezinski had doubts about West Germany's trade with the East, especially the provision of state-backed export credit insurance. Perhaps the upshot of the Venice meeting is best conveyed by the 6/23/80 FAZ cartoon in which a sour-looking Mr. Schmidt is unwillingly shaking hands with Mr. Carter and urging, "Drop me another line, Jimmy!"

As a postscript, Mr. Schmidt went to Moscow, strongly criticized the Russians over Afghanistan in a Kremlin banquet speech, defended the NATO missiles decision, and extracted what seemed to be a concession from the Russians. Moscow indicated that it was willing to talk with the West on the missiles without insisting, as it had hitherto, that the December NATO decision first be revoked. Comments on 7/2 and 7/3/80 in the FAZ—that is, before details of the results of Mr. Schmidt's Kremlin bargaining were announced—revealed the newspaper's continuing skepticism. In one the Moscow visit was linked (for neither the first nor the last time) to the forthcoming West German general election on 10/15/80—the suggestion being that Mr. Schmidt needed, or at least wanted, a foreign policy success for domestic reasons.

A thorough and well-balanced correspondent's report from Bonn in the 7/4/80 FAZ gave details both of Mr. Schmidt's Bundestag speech and of the tough criticism by the opposition leader, Franz Josef Strauss. Mr. Schmidt said, "It is important that a new situation has been created," but also added, "I don't consider this to be a breakthrough yet." Mr. Strauss claimed that the Moscow trip came at an inappropriate time and was "superficial and dangerous." "The West will have to pay the political alimony in the long run," according to Mr. Strauss, for the small concessions which Mr. Schmidt gained. To close this episode, Jan Reifenberg reported from Washington on 7/4/80 that Mr. Carter had expressed admiration for Mr. Schmidt's achievement. Reifenberg also noted, however, that the State Department was carefully studying the apparent concession from Moscow to see if there was, in fact, anything new in it.

Neither side seemed to emerge from this very well. Mr. Schmidt's original comments were susceptible to misinterpretation. Mr. Carter either did not receive or ignored Mr. Schmidt's explanation of what he had meant. Both sides sought to convey their real feelings to one another via newspapers, which naturally gives the press a certain ironic satisfaction. But it is obviously worrying that such failures of communication and comprehension are possible between two key allies at so dangerous a period of world affairs. What about those hot lines, red telephones, aides, and experts? What are the ambassadors up to, and if they are performing their duties well, why does their work apparently make so little impact when the most serious issues are at stake between the most important people? Why was it impossible for Western leaders to get together before the convenient excuse of an economic summit to discuss strategy in the face of Iran and Afghanistan? This is no time for finger pointing, still less for a witch hunt. But it seems urgently necessary to establish how the mistakes of this year can be avoided in the future.

With the categories on European-American relations and intermediate-range missiles dealt with in detail, and some lessons explicitly drawn from them, the other topics can be covered fairly briefly.

Most notable in the military reporting of the FAZ over these months were the articles by Adalbert Weinstein. Two of them, carrying the headlines, "NATO—a Fair Weather Alliance?" on 4/19/80, and "Sleeping NATO" on 5/17/80, characterized the note of concern that ran through almost all of Weinstein's reports. The picture was one of an alliance apparently incapable of responding quickly to the threat posed by Iran and Afghanistan, one in which, moreover, the member countries were ever more ready to decide their defense policy according to fiscal rather than strategic criteria. Mr. Weinstein was worried about the NATO alliance, especially about its flexible-response doctrine, and he thought that the alliance's sickness stemmed from weak American leadership.

There are four points to make. The first is that Mr. Weinstein's military knowledge is clearly wide and his analysis is disturbing. The second is that NATO has been under criticism from its member states since its foundation. There seems almost never to have been a time when it was not in some sort of crisis. Yet it is still there (though only just, if one interprets the trend of Mr. Weinstein's articles correctly). Third, at least one member country—Britain—earned the praise of the FAZ in a 6/19/80 editorial for its readiness to install nuclear missiles on its soil without jawing with the Russians. In contrast to the Federal Republic, said the FAZ, the United Kingdom was not afraid to state its intentions loudly and clearly. Fourth, the prospect mentioned in the FAZ of 6/9/80 that France might develop and deploy the neutron weapon is clearly of major importance to European allies facing the Warsaw Pact's numerical superiority in tank forces. That goes for West Germany in particular.

For Category Five, covering Iran and the Middle East, I can mention only four pieces from a snow of articles. The first is a report on 4/24/80 by the indefatigable Mr. Stadlmann, this time in Luxembourg, about the EEC's slowness in applying economic sanctions and called, "Has Europe once again left itself an open back door?" This well illustrated the way in which the Germans were pressing for decision, but finally had to accept footdragging. Connoisseurs of EEC procedure will like the description of how a proposal to impose sanctions by a set date, "if the hostages are not freed by then," was rejected, its substitute being a proposal to act only "if decisive progress" toward freeing the hostages could not be shown to have been achieved by that date.

The second article is by Mr. Rene Wagner from Riad, stressing that the Saudi Arabians wanted no U.S. military presence in the Persian Gulf. This piece appeared on 4/8/80, two months before both a visit to Bonn by the Saudi king and foreign minister and the announcement in Venice of the EEC's Middle East initiative. Was this EEC step a help or a hindrance to the United States' own Middle East peace efforts?

In an editorial called "Risky Dialogue" on 7/23/80, the FAZ expressed fears (shared by many in Bonn, including part of the SPD) that the EEC might simply be complicating an already difficult situation. The editorial suggested that sometimes "a stalled front is better than movement in the wrong direction," and it expressed the hope that the Bonn government would not "burn its fingers"—or worse—through its involvement in the Middle East question.

Finally, Mr. Weinstein again, with one of the best background articles I have seen on the American attempt to rescue the Teheran hostages and the reasons for failure; it was carried in the 4/28/80 edition. The FAZ criticized the rescue enterprise more in sorrow than in anger. "No time to throw stones," is how one of its editorials put it.

On the Olympic boycott issue, the West Germans were again the European pacemakers (although that pace still seemed too slow for Washington's liking). The Bonn government's arguments to the athletes against going to the Moscow games, the clear vote of the German National Olympic Committee to stay at home, and the (reluctant) admiration of some other European states that did not decide in the same way—all were carried in great detail on both the political and sporting pages in the FAZ.

Less impressive, according to the newspaper, was the German attitude toward business with the East. Were only athletes to make the sacrifices because of Afghanistan, asked Jürgen Jeske in a 7/26/80 editorial? No doubt some Americans (including Mr. Brzezinski?) asked themselves the same question when they read Klaus Broichausen's article," Moscow wants to talk business with Schmidt." This was written on 6/25/80, five days before the chancellor's talks in the Soviet capital were to begin. The signing of a West German–Soviet long-term economic accord and the formal go ahead for negotiations on a huge natural gas deal were in prospect. The Germans appeared to have stuck to their commitment not to take up business with the Soviet Union lost to U.S. firms because of President Carter's post-Afghanistan embargo decision. But they were also clearly determined to use to the full what scope they had beyond the terms of this commitment to intensify economic links with the East. Was this wise? Did Mr. Schmidt's Moscow trip help make the Russians "respectable" again after Afghanistan while bringing the West relatively little in return? In a series of editorials, the FAZ made it clear that it felt this to be the case. Robert Held on 7/4/80 said that Americans still heed the adage not to bargain unless you have something with which to negotiate: Washington does not view Schmidt's "concessions" from the Soviets to negotiate about middle-range rockets as a Trojan horse, but it remains cautious.

And so to the domestic scene in the United States, and first the election campaign. Reviewing the FAZ's coverage of America's internal politics is important not only to recognize its excellence, but to describe the picture that German readers get from the FAZ of their transatlantic ally—the perceptions that can be crucial to public support for alliance policies. There were four main questions that Europeans were likely to raise about the U.S. election, all of which the FAZ coverage answered well.

First, who was involved in addition to the incumbent president? There were plenty of pieces about the Reagans, but an article on John Anderson by Jan Reifenberg that appeared on 6/3/80 did a particularly good job in presenting (for a European) a relatively unknown figure—his personality and prospects combined with a little American history too.

The second question was, how were the candidates doing? The running coverage of this did not disappoint, whether on the fates of George Bush and Ted Kennedy or on the likely impact of affairs like "Billygate." If a sense of drama often seemed lacking, no doubt the campaign itself was much to blame.

The third question was, what would Mr. Reagan's foreign policy stance probably be if he came to power? Mr. Reifenberg's article of 7/11/80, "Back to the Fifties?," did not fill me with optimism, but it was partly encouraging to learn that Mr. Reagan had several competent advisers who recognized that reestablishment of a "pax Americana" was not the answer to everything.

Finally, what of the U.S. economy and what impact, if any, was being made on policy by the election campaign? The answer was mixed. On the one hand Ms. Carola Kaps produced a bullish article on 4/12/80 about "Signs of first success in American energy policy." President Carter was firmly praised for putting the country, virtually against its will, on the right energy road. The comparative record of the United States on reducing use of energy in recent years was also praised. An article by Ms. Kaps dated 8/18/80 called "Economic policy confusion," however, raised familiar fears. Could Mr. Carter bring in the kind of program to boost the economy that he promised at the Democratic convention without increasing inflation? Were there clear signs of how U.S. productivity could be improved? An FAZ report datelined Boston and giving details of an economics discussion at Harvard suggested that many informed Americans were themselves skeptical.

Two final points. First, while I feel there was enough coverage of broad economic and financial policy in the FAZ, I can well imagine that German businessmen (increasingly involved in the American market) would like more reports both on their American competitors and on the labor setup. (Ms. Kaps' report of 6/9/80 on trade unions and German firms in the United States was an honorable exception here.)

Second, the article of 5/9/80 datelined Frankfurt called "How fast do prices really rise" is worth its weight in gold at least. It details what one has long suspected—that any comparison of inflation rates in West Germany and the United States that does not take account of the different methods used to arrive at the figures is virtually worthless. Yet much business and governmental judgment appears to be based on the assumption that the methods used for calculation are the same in both countries.

And so back to the point at which I began—culture, tourism, and the American "way of life"—with a quotation from an article by Peter Odrich datelined Los Angeles, 5/22/80: "It's really strange," a taxi driver is quoted as saying, "the whole world insults America but everyone wants to go there." The piece describes some of the California arrivals: the refugees from Southeast Asia, the university entrants from Middle Eastern countries, well-to-do European couples worried about war or some other crisis at home. Everyone's dream seems to be a big house with lots of land, and of course a view of the Pacific Ocean.

Virtually any Saturday edition of the FAZ supports these observations. Advertisements tempting Germans to buy farms in California jostle with information about cheap flights to Miami or Atlanta. Presumably it pays to insert them. The sight of it all helps to keep the transatlantic political differences in perspective.

So does the article on the composer Ernst Krenek (datelined Palm Springs in April) who fled Austria in 1938, found refuge in America, and seems to have his works performed much more often in the United States these days than in Europe. The piece underlines the range and vitality of the arts in America, a fact that seems to me to make insufficient impact either in the FAZ or in any other European newspaper I know. It is also a reminder that the United States offered a home to many Europeans when they had nowhere else to go. One should not need to jog memories about that, but perhaps one must all the same.

Finally, back to Europe and to an outstanding series of articles by Mr. Gillessen in July on the life of American GIs in the Federal Republic. Here (7/29/80) is another taxi driver—a German this time—complaining that, years before, Americans used to treat him with as little regard as the dollar bill they tossed in payment. Today, the driver notes happily, the dollar is weak, the Americans are poor, he is treated with more respect—and that is much better.

The series is thoroughly researched and very well observed. Many Germans have surely read it with profit and, no doubt, astonishment at discovering problems under their noses of which they had been only dimly aware. If I were inclined to pick out the top contribution from the more than 600 pieces considered here, then this would be my choice.

Response to Carr

The Schmidt-FAZ Affair

A Bonn government press official suggested that Chancellor Schmidt took such offense at the FAZ's coverage of his comments linking the installation of new missiles to the start of arms negotiations not because of the initial confusion, but because when Schmidt later explained in special press briefings what he had meant, the proper message was still not conveyed to the German public, or to opinion leaders in the United States. Schmidt attacked the FAZ, according to this account, in order to stir so much attention that at last he would be rightly understood.

The FAZ's own Jan Reifenberg ventured that, given such an incident, the best journalistic response was "the Anglo-Saxon way: get the facts—don't comment." In this particular case, it was his understanding that Brzezinski was worried that the whole discussion over the deployment of intermediate-range missiles in Europe might lead dangerously to a delay or reversal of commitments. "It was a classic case," Reifenberg said, "of the problems of interpretation between Bonn and the U.S., stemming partly from Germany's characteristic nervousness. It is still true, 'If Washington coughs, Bonn gets pneumonia.' "

The friction that grew between Schmidt and the FAZ seemed exceptional to Murray Seeger, the *Los Angeles Times'* correspondent in Brussels, who suggested that, more commonly, the German press "doesn't challenge or question" the official statements it is given. "It's easy there," he said, "to give a secret speech"—that is, for a leading politician to propose a policy initiative in public, which is then neither examined nor even reported in the press.

The FAZ's Günther Gillessen would not accept that this was true for his own newspaper. With Schmidt, it had been both challenging and questioning. Gillessen admitted that the FAZ may have overestimated the apparent change in Schmidt's position in that instance, but he asked, "How could the Chancellor have trusted the extemporaneous occasion of a political speech in Hamburg—where no member of the Bonn press corps, which follows national and international affairs, would be present—to make so important a foreign policy overture?" While the FAZ may have relied too much on what it received as a verbatim record ("though still unclear") of Schmidt's speech, Gillessen said that even after attempts at clarification, Schmidt's position was "still an ambivalent thing." Summing up the FAZ's view, Gillessen stated, "Schmidt overstated the prospect for arms limitation."

A spokesman for Schmidt agreed that the chancellor's initial statement was made under less than ideal circumstances ("Only local journalists were present"), but defended Schmidt's subsequent efforts to put the matter right.

To an observer from the United States, the astonishing feature of the Schmidt-FAZ affair was that both sides attributed a great deal of the confusion to the fact that Schmidt had made his comments in Hamburg, not in Bonn! From the FAZ's viewpoint, such a speech was too important to be given to "local" journalists—and without advance notice of its content. From the chancellor's viewpoint, the instinctive retort was not, "Why didn't you send your national affairs correspondents to Hamburg?" but rather, "Given the unfavorable circumstances of the first speech, why weren't you satisfied with the later explanations we made especially for you?"

To note how countries can differ in their tacit rules of the relationship between the press and the head of government, one need only imagine how it would be received if an incumbent American president running for reelection, on complaining that a speech he delivered in Chicago was misreported, was told, "It's your fault for giving it there when all the knowledgable reporters are in Washington." Or imagine still further the president's replying, "Well, you're right, Chicago was the wrong setting, but then you shouldn't pay attention to what I said there when I was perfectly willing to tell you exactly what I meant back here in Washington."

At least two things are amiss in that imaginary incident. For one, if the president went to Chicago, most of the White House press corps would go there, too. And for another, explaining afterward what the president really meant is usually left to subordinates.

The FAZ's Influence

Peter Galliner, Director of the International Press Institute, Zurich/London, put aside the FAZ-Schmidt affair to describe the place of the FAZ among other German newspapers and periodicals. The FAZ has achieved, Galliner said, an impressive breadth represented by its own network of correspondents. They are better, he judged, than those of any other German-language paper, and they are given both the space and the encouragement to express their own views. This largely accounts, he said, for the FAZ's "great influence abroad."

Galliner also pointed out that the FAZ's signed editorials represent the writer's opinion; they should not be taken as the official position of the newspaper. In this, he said, the FAZ is an exception in Germany. Its independence is in contrast, for example, to *Die Zeit,* the weekly opinion journal that specifically expresses and supports the views of Schmidt and his government, politically if not economically.

The FAZ's coverage of the movement in Poland to establish independent trade unions—and of the tensions this created between Poland and other Warsaw Pact countries, especially the Soviet Union—prompted different reactions. While observing that the FAZ reported the subject "with almost disconcerting diligence," Jonathan Carr found reason to be critical. In an FAZ editorial, Fritz Ulrich Fack had pointed to the apparently worsening Polish situation as evidence of the failure of *Ostpolitik,* Germany's active policy to open lines of mutual accommodation with the East. Fack had argued that a policy that depended for its success on a permanent relaxation of tensions would surely lead to tragic disappointment.

"But what alternative is available?" Carr asked. The FAZ, he felt, had not gone beyond its questioning of current policy to suggest something different. It had paid too little attention, for example, to the economic assistance that might be offered the Poles. "Is it just a matter of letting them stew in their own juice?" he asked, "or should one investigate and address the *consequences* of doing that as opposed to lending them a hand?"

Taking issue with Carr, Melvin Lasky, Editor of *Encounter,* said that if he were to fault Fack's editorial on the failure of *Ostpolitik,* it would be because Fack's was only "a *moderate* summing up of the facts." Lasky professed to agree "with 95 percent of what the FAZ says," finding less to criticize in its record than in what he called "the shocking fact that the FAZ has so little influence." His explanation for this alleged failing was that most German intellectuals belong to the liberal-left way of thinking and therefore discount the FAZ as a "voice of conservatism." FAZ's only journalistic problem, he thought, was that it sometimes misses stories it should do—for example, "What were the ambassadors doing while Schmidt and Brzezinski were tilting with each other in the press? Is nothing communicated at their level any more?"

Reifenberg, speaking from his experience of being posted abroad, said that the FAZ had become "markedly domestic in its range of concerns, very conservative in its politics." This could frustrate someone in his position: "I don't see the FAZ's editorials until some days after they are written and often have to ask myself, 'For God's sake, why didn't the guy call me?' " He was less inclined than Lasky to fault ambassadors for failing to maintain their traditional importance in policy communications between nations: "The fault is in their leaders who choose to use today's instantaneous means of communication to go right over their heads." That sort of direct communication between heads of government, Reifenberg implied, can exacerbate as well as assuage the tendencies toward divisiveness, particularly if one of the principals is prone to changes of mind—as Carter was, for example, on whether to deploy the neutron bomb in Europe. The shaking of confidence, when it occurs between figures at the highest level, cannot then be excused as a mis-understanding among subordinates.

A Bonn government press official confirmed the view that the FAZ addressed mostly Christian Democratic (CDU) voters, its attitude being closer to the opposition's than to the current government's, and so for that reason enjoyed less influence than it might. This representative of the ruling Social Democratic (SPD) and Free Democratic (FDP) coalition maintained that the FAZ tended to be pro–U.S. and critical of Germany's policy conduct.

Gerhard Kunz, a member of the Bundestag (Germany's parliament), allowed that the *facts* researched and reported by the FAZ are "usually correct, indeed, the most reliable source of background in Germany." On the question of political stance, he said, "Lots of people are glad there is *one* newspaper that *is* concerned with the future of good relations between Germany and the U.S., while the others lean toward saying, 'We're grown up and we don't have to listen to the U.S. so much any more.' " With this in mind, Kunz thought that the FAZ's coverage of the relations between Schmidt and Reagan should prove particularly interesting; he was "not sure all will be well on the issues."

The FAZ's Governance

An FAZ publisher, Joachim Fest, explained that some of the newspaper's claim to a reputation for independence—or at least of diversity—stems from the differences among its sections. The cultural department, represented in the FAZ's third section, operates "a little more like a forum" as compared with the first section of political affairs.

More importantly, as described in Carr's review, the structure providing for ownership and decision making is unique to the FAZ. Sixty-eight percent of the FAZ's ownership shares are held by a foundation that plays a decidedly retiring role. Its board meets just once a year to hear a report. The other shares are held by private individuals including the persons who serve as the publishers *(Herausgebers)*. The publishers being also the editorial board, they meet weekly to discuss not only personnel assignments but also the policy line of the newspaper, and they take part in other conferences almost daily. The chairmanship rotates among them every year. This is a departure from other papers that may have similar boards but have a chairman who does not change regularly and therefore effectively becomes editor-in-chief. Thus, the antagonism that is historic to so many newspapers is eliminated in the FAZ: the owners and editors are the same.

"Everyone must be envious of the FAZ's greatness," Lasky declared. "How was it achieved? First, it has had an unparalleled run—ten, fifteen years—in opposition to the government: that's always the best position for a newspaper. Second, it enjoys, being in Germany, a national fetish for *long* pieces—the writers have room to move around in. Given any FAZ article, I always read the last paragraph first; if it's interesting, then I go back and work my way through all the argument. If *The New York Times* tried the same thing, its circulation wouldn't be 900,000: it would be only 90,000. And if *The Times* in London tried it, it would be in worse financial trouble."

Other German newspapers boast higher circulations than the FAZ's 330,000, but the FAZ has built up a profitable business. Its appeal is to a reading public that seems, among the countries included in this study, disproportionately interested in fact-filled, carefully-argued writing. This perhaps natural advantage over the newspapers in the United States, Britain, and France is braced by the FAZ's novel governing and editorial structure.

The industrial and political leaders who established the FAZ managed to include a set of publisher-editors with whom they were in close sympathy. These *Herausgebers* were then, and remain, entrusted to develop and run the FAZ as if they were the sole owners. One supposes that this arrangement, which has succeeded so admirably both in sponsoring journalism of a high standard and in making a profit, could be upset in the event of a fundamental rift in political outlook between the *Herausgebers* and those who sit on the board that holds most of the FAZ's shares in trust—or in the event of such a rift among the *Herausgebers* themselves. It hasn't happened yet, and the years of stable management already achieved may constitute a tradition that will help to prevent it in the future. Meanwhile, the effect of this institutional novelty may be seen from abroad as a happy oddity. The very cohesiveness in political philosophy that characterizes the managers of the FAZ, and that is generally recognized in Germany to support the conservative line, has made possible the flourishing of a newspaper that is relied on by readers all along the political spectrum.

—MR

chapter two

THE NEW YORK TIMES:
Making Importance Popular

Jan Reifenberg *

Founded in 1851, *The New York Times* enjoyed early success, then declined, only to be reinvigorated starting in 1896 by its new owner and publisher, Adolph Simon Ochs, whose drive to provide the most comprehensive news coverage built the reputation that the newspaper carries on today. Ochs' son-in-law, Arthur Hays Sulzberger, became publisher upon Ochs' death in 1935 and continued in the position until 1961. Two years later, his son, Arthur Ochs ("Punch") Sulzberger took over at the age of 37, and almost immediately inaugurated changes in the editors' ranks, followed in the '70s by the establishment of new insert sections for each day of the week ("Weekend," "Living," etc.) and a variety of technological innovations in the newsroom and the printing process. While not always pleasing to its longtime readers, these and other changes in *The New York Times* are credited with helping to keep the newspaper profitable and its circulation rising.†

T*he New York Times* is the most respected daily newspaper in the United States. It can be called an institution. At a time when foreign coverage on an exclusive basis has, in most other American newspapers, diminished to a mere trickle (and news from Europe has become almost nonexistent on all major American television networks with the exception of "on the spot" event coverage), *The New York Times* maintains by far the largest staff of full-time foreign correspondents. They work exclusively for the paper and its syndicated news services.

---

*Washington Correspondent, *Frankfurter Allgemeine Zeitung*

†John C. Merrill and Harold A. Fisher, *The World's Great Dailies* (New York: Hastings House, 1980), pp. 220–230.

The readers of *The New York Times* should be able on a continuous basis to form an objective, largely independent view of events abroad and their relationship to U.S. policies and, indeed, to the readers' own lives. The slogan, "All the news that's fit to print," would seem to guarantee such a possibility, since it remains the high standard for the journalists who work for *The New York Times*.

Yet it cannot be said that *The New York Times'* coverage of U.S.-European relations during the period from April 4 to September 3, 1980, fulfilled all of one's expectations of consistent observation. The pattern of emphasis upon events, countries, or personalities was uneven in ways that could not always have been dictated by the demands of a crucial "spot event," but seemed instead to reflect particular wishes, feelings, or even prejudices of the editorial staff or the individual correspondent.

It is important to bear in mind the main factors that influenced relations between the United States and Europe during this period:

• The developments and attitudes with respect to the crises in Iran and Afghanistan and their consequences;
• Efforts to increase NATO's security while at the same time maintaining a modicum of contact with the Soviet Union in order to salvage future arms control negotiations and what was left of "détente"; and
• The effects of the workers' strike in Poland in August.

On both sides of the Atlantic, domestic political influences had a strong bearing upon policy attitudes. In the United States, the presidential election campaign, as always, influenced Washington's foreign and security policies to a great extent. It seems legitimate to ask whether a series of pertinent developments—such as the Olympic boycott or the efforts to impose sanctions against the USSR in response to its invasion of Afghanistan or against Iran for the seizure of American hostages in Teheran—were viewed in Washington more in the context of winning or losing the election in November than as realistic levers on the behavior of foreign powers.

It is self-evident, for instance, that the timing for leaks to the press about the president's directive for a "countervailing" nuclear strategy was chosen in August primarily to counter Governor Reagan's polemics against President Carter's defense policy. It seems just as evident that the White House, prior to the Venice summit, deliberately leaked information about profound differences of opinion between President Carter and Chancellor Schmidt regarding the modernization of theater nuclear forces in Western Europe. And it seemed that the effort to counter a widespread European perception of Carter's alleged weakness in leadership overwhelmed, at least at times, the ability to cope with the concrete problems at hand.

Apart from the search for answers to the Soviet occupation of Afghanistan, the hostage taking in Iran, and the workers' strikes in Poland, an old dispute continued, namely, whether the American security guarantees for Western Europe were still valid and to what extent the European allies should, or could, entrust their survival to the hands of the president of the United States. Should they, by enlarging their national forces and maintaining a degree of national independence, try to steer a more individual course, thus safeguarding their energy resources in the Middle East and the rewards of "détente" with the Soviet Union and their other Eastern European neighbors? Another perennial aspect of Atlantic relations that came up again was the question of how much consultation there should be between Washington and the European allies.

The American presidential election campaign was a critical influence upon the whole of the relationship, politically as well as psychologically. One naturally wonders how much it promoted, or slowed down, developments arising from other causes that should have been dealt with pragmatically in their own terms. Certain developments—the energy crisis, relations with oil-producing countries of the Middle East, the facts and consequences of strategic and regional defense in the nuclear age, internal questions of such grave importance as the Polish strikes or the fate and future of Yugoslavia after Tito's death—ought not, among policy makers, to be seen in exclusive correlation with the vagaries of an American election campaign. But the 1980 campaign, which was in full swing at the time this review was submitted, provoked, to a greater degree than its predecessors, a line of thinking in Europe that could be summarized thus: Can and should one depend upon a country which, every four years at least, seems to deviate from pragmatic foreign policy for the benefit of selecting a new president? Is that system still viable?

Looking at *The New York Times'* coverage of U.S.–European relations during this period is, in many ways, like looking at a mirror of such thoughts and questions. It is by necessity a partial mirror. The best that can be said about it is that it reflects the present state of transatlantic affairs, which is unfortunately—and in spite of official disclaimers of varied conviction—characterized by a drifting apart, both political and intellectual.

How this highly influential newspaper in the East Coast metropolis chooses European topics—from the relative weight it gives to specific events, trends, or personalities—shows a certain parochialism. To the trained eye, the selection of a topic, the space given to a particular correspondent, the placement of his or her story in the paper all indicate the degree of interest and importance that editors give to the topic. It must be said that in *The New York Times* European news often appears to be treated either as a reflection of American interests or according to the "spot interest" of a particular editor in New York.

Despite its professed independence and objectivity, *The New York Times* reflects, moreover, official thinking in Washington so closely as to raise a fundamental question: To what degree must a newspaper maintain a healthy distance from government? This question is especially pertinent in an era when the huge public relations machinery of interested government agencies and departments purposely floods the media with an incessant stream of tendentious information.

Interestingly, *The New York Times'* news from Eastern Europe (with the exception of the USSR) was by far more extensive than its news from Western European countries even before the events in Poland became the main story. General European developments—that is, facts, influence, or planning of the European Economic Community (EEC) as well as European attitudes toward economic sanctions—dominated the period before, during, and shortly after the Venice summit. Yet the reader of *The New York Times* would, with one notable exception, have searched in vain for a truly comprehensive analysis of the EEC's political, let alone its economic, importance.

As an observer of the United States for a number of years, this reviewer is struck by the fact that *The New York Times* seems generally reluctant to admit that the postwar American attitude toward Europe must change its character from that of the unquestionably dominant power to that of equal partner (at least economically), if the relationship is to be valid and healthy for the benefit of all partners of the alliance.

A few quantitative facts (summarized in Table 2.1) seem particularly interesting to this analyst. Between April 4 and September 3, 1980, there appeared a grand total of 96 front-page stories from or related to Europe in *The New York Times*. Of these, 33 concerned Eastern Europe (excluding the Soviet Union); 29 related to the question of sanctions, East-West relations, and the Venice summit; only eight related to the Federal Republic of Germany, considered to be Washington's most important ally in NATO; seven related to the USSR; six each to the United Kingdom and to NATO; three to France; three to the vast area of Southern and Southeastern Europe; and one to Scandinavia.

During the same period, there appeared a total of only 19 editorials with reference to European topics. Only eight rated top placement. Six editorials related to the problems and questions of the Venice summit; another related to the Moscow Olympics; five dealt with the workers' strikes in Poland; three concerned Turkey; two, the United Kingdom; one, Spain; and one, questions of international terrorism. Measured

Table 2.1. The New York Times' Prominent Coverage of U.S.-European Relations: April 4 to September 3, 1980.

Subject	Front-Page News Stories	Editorials
Eastern Europe (excluding the Soviet Union)	33	5
East-West relations, the question of sanctions on the Soviet Union, and the Venice Summit	29	7
Federal Republic of Germany	8	
Soviet Union	7	
United Kingdom	6	2
NATO	6	
France	3	
Southern and Southeastern Europe	3	3
Scandinavia	1	
Spain		1
International terrorism		1
Total	**96**	**19**

against the importance of European-American relations, this is quite astonishing: European problems (and their relationship to the United States) rated an average of only 3.8 editorials per month.

A most notable and commendable distinction was provided by the "Foreign Affairs" columns of Flora Lewis. She continues the tradition of Anne O'Hare McCormick and Cyrus L. Sulzberger brilliantly. She has an uncanny feeling for the importance of news and developments. She always goes to places where there is not only action to be found, but future trends to be seen. Moreover, she has a sense of history that seems absent from most other *New York Times* news stories.

Here now are several short analyses of European-related news and comments in *The New York Times,* grouped according to the following order of topics:

• General relations with the European Economic Community (including the question of political and economic sanctions, the Venice summit and its aftermath);

• Questions relating to NATO, to arms control negotiations, and to general European strategy;
• Relations with the Federal Republic of Germany;
• Relations with the Soviet Union;
• Relations with Eastern Europe (excluding the USSR);
• Relations with the United Kingdom;
• Relations with France;
• Relations with Southern and Southeastern Europe;
• Relations with Scandinavia;
• Editorials.

Relations with the European Economic Community

General relations between the United States and Europe, in particular with the EEC, figured prominently in *The New York Times*. James Reston (4/9/80) described President Carter's dilemma in trying to mesh his reelection strategy with his foreign policy and the problems this created for transatlantic relations:

> The more moves he [Carter] makes on Iran or Afghanistan that may appeal to the voters at home, the less support he seems to get from the allies. . . .
>
> The conflict between the Carter Administration and the Soviet Union over the Red Army's invasion of Afghanistan, and the conflict between Washington and Teheran over the hostages have exposed what is probably a more fundamental conflict between the United States and its allies in Europe and Japan. They respect Mr. Carter's condemnation of Soviet aggression and his sanctions against Iran, but while they support his principles, they have more vital economic and political interests in Iran and the other Mideast oil-producers than the United States, and more important economic ties to the U.S.S.R.
>
> For example, the Federal Republic in West Germany exports almost twice as much to the Soviet Union as the United States. American exports to the U.S.S.R. and its East European allies amount to 2.1 percent of our export trade, while West Germany's amount to 5.7 percent of its trade. This helps explain why Chancellor Schmidt is not very enthusiastic about joining Carter in sanctions against Moscow or in boycotting the Moscow Olympics.

Flora Lewis, in "The Week in Review" (4/20/80), wrote a thorough analysis of the dilemma in which the Europeans found themselves prior to the meetings with Secretary of State Muskie at Vienna and with the president at the Venice summit:

> There is, in all this [Iran, Afghanistan, etc.], a whiff of the deep fear of vulnerability which brought about the alliance in the first place. There are also vital differences, nearly two generations later, including a perception

of vastly increased Soviet strength, a reduced confidence in the capacity and wisdom of the United States after Vietnam and its domestic conse- quences, a feeling that the remoteness of the crisis spots (well outside NATO territory) should allow Europe to escape unscathed, and above all, an awareness that the Europeans have developed interests which diverge from Washington's. The divergence ranges from such immediate facts as the nationality of the hostages in Teheran, through trade that is often com- petitive with the United States and lucratively complementary with the Soviet Union.

The only large, comprehensive description of the effects of the Soviet invasion of Afghanistan upon Europe was a *New York Times Magazine* piece, "Europe Cashes in on Carter's Cold War" (4/27/80) by James O. Goldsborough. The author worked for many years as a foreign corre- spondent in Paris. Here was one rare example of an observer who had ample time to study, comprehend, and evaluate European attitudes while maintaining his own critical viewpoint. He went deeply into the reasons *why* Europe was tending to act more independently.

Washington's irritation at the limits to the economic sanctions which the EEC adopted against Iran and at the secretly prepared meeting be- tween French President Giscard d'Estaing and Soviet President Brezhnev at Warsaw was quite evident in Bernard Gwertzman's lead stories (5/20 and 5/21/80). Gwertzman usually reflected the prevailing attitudes at the Department of State, especially its planning staff, and also the thinking of the Secretary of State—for example (5/20/80):

> Mr. Muskie, in referring to France's secrecy over the Warsaw meeting, reflected some personal irritation by saying:
> "I'm concerned that when I was being given a lecture on consultation, that the lecturer was not inclined to practice what he was preaching."

James Reston, in his column (5/23/80), wrote a clear analysis in which he tried to explain why President Carter seemed to have lost the confidence of the allies who "support him more in public, fearing Mr. Reagan, than they do in private":

> Moreover, they are puzzled by Mr. Carter. One day he wants sanctions against Iran, and then withdraws them, and then calls on everybody to impose them later on. He opposes talks by Cyrus Vance with Soviet Foreign Minister Gromyko, then agrees to talks with Gromyko by his new Secretary of State, Edmund Muskie, and then is angry when the President of France talks to President Brezhnev in Poland without prior consultation.

The amount of European apprehension over the presidential election in the United States and the motives for a series of misunderstandings during the Carter years were the subject of a column by Flora Lewis (6/10/80) in which she came to the conclusion that "it is time for them [the Europeans] to accept that they can and should share the responsibilities of leadership. Then they would have less to cavil at or fear from any American President."

The factual reporting of R. W. Apple on the Western European leaders' meeting at Venice prior to the summit was commendable. He explained the difficulties, while Flora Lewis in a column, "Europe Lolls at the Brink" (6/13/80), described what seemed to her to be ambivalent reasons for the EEC's stand on the Palestinian question:

> In the circumstances, a fairly anodynic European stand is emerging, at least for the time being, repeating acceptance of Palestinian "self-determination," mentioning the "problem" of Jerusalem without saying what to do about it, and calling for further "Euro-Arab dialogue" between representatives of the Community and the Arab League. That constitutes admission that however impatient the Europeans are with Israel, and with the United States, there is nothing more productive they can do now to ease the Middle East conflict or even further their own interests with the oil producers.
>
> Still, they have reached a degree of consensus which makes them likely to act if they do see a chance for effect, whether or not the U.S. agrees. This bodes more European-American friction in the future, a new kind of Washington lobby out to counter the American Jewish lobby which Europeans denounce nowadays almost as vehemently as Arabs do.

Henry Tanner, *The New York Times'* correspondent in Rome, then (6/14/80) gave the factual description of the EEC's Venice declaration on the Middle East. The verbatim text of the declaration also appeared. The reader was well informed about a decision that had strong impact on the U.S.–European relationship. That preceded another analysis ("The Week in Review," 6/15/80) by Flora Lewis, "Europe as a Third Force?" These quotations show her grasp of world affairs:

> The Europeans do have a presence and a capacity to deal with some Arab states that are scarcely on speaking terms with the United States. That would be a contribution to the West, they argue, not a subversion of American peacemaking efforts; the argument might be more persuasive if they did more to help Egypt's Anwar el-Sadat break out of isolation. . . .
>
> But the crucial test for Europe comes in the relation with the Soviet Union. Every European country has its gamut of opinion, crudely described as ranging from pro- to anti-American. More properly, the issues are perceived as each country's welfare and survival and how to assure them. . . .
>
> The overriding issue is East-West relations and the meaning for security. No longer does this mean just the heavily armed front dividing Europe, the

military ratio. Europeans are acutely aware that it also means economic and political stability of other regions, supply routes and the flow of oil and raw materials. There is a fairly general assumption that Moscow's objective in Western Europe is not conquest or direct dominion, but the acquisition of a docile, if independent, productive backyard sufficiently detached from United States influence to provide reliable compensation for Communist bloc economic failures. This European view further suggests that the Soviet Union seeks to use its frightening military shadow to control vital avenues of supply, as the means of forcing that role on Western Europe.

The extent to which *The New York Times* quite often reflects White House thinking was shown in Bernard Gwertzman's stories during President Carter's trip to the Venice summit. His article, "What Kind of Alliance Is This, Anyway?" ("The Week in Review," 6/22/80), portrayed the differences of opinion and approach between Carter and his European counterparts:

> At a state dinner in Rome on Friday, President Carter set the tone for today's meeting, warning the allies, though not by name, that Europe could not be "an island of detente" while the Russians were in Afghanistan. "To assume that aggression need be met only when it occurs at one's own doorstep is to tempt new and very serious adventures," Mr. Carter said. . . . the Administration's reigning foreign policy thinker, Zbigniew Brzezinski, views the Europeans' reluctance to punish the Soviet Union as analogous to the appeasement of Hitler that led to World War II. Reporters were also reminded before taking off last week that Venice, once Europe's mightiest city-state, collapsed after it failed to go to the defense of Constantinople against the expansionist Turks in the 15th century.
> Such analogies fall on skeptical ears in Western Europe, where detente has become a way of life. This is especially true in West Germany, where the Social Democrats came to power 11 years ago on the promise of improving relations with Moscow as a means of easing the lot of East Germans and ethnic Germans in the Soviet Union and Poland. After returning from the Venice conference, Mr. Schmidt will barely have time to unpack before he flies to Moscow for a meeting with Leonid I. Brezhnev next week.

In the same issue, *The New York Times'* correspondent, John Vinocur, wrote ("Mr. Schmidt Wanted a Word with Herr Carter") about the reasons for the divergent attitudes toward sanctions and East-West affairs that prevailed before the chancellor met again with the president:

> His [Schmidt's] answer to growing risks where the West is weak, is to bolster the independence of the third world, which would require much help and patience from the United States. The emphasis would be on basic assistance rather than military help. . . .

Finally, the West Germans contend that to permit proper concentration on the developing countries, vigorous efforts must be made to block new tensions in Europe. . . .

It is here that Mr. Schmidt's arguments seem to run most sharply counter to United States thinking. Discussing the West's strategic options recently, an American policy maker indicated that he did not share West German optimism about the possibility of exerting a steadying influence on the third world. He saw only limited chances for successful Western intervention in third world crises over the next decade. The West's best dissuasive mechanism, he said, is in Western Europe, the region where it is strongest and where the Soviet Union has the most to lose. The question, he said, was whether the European allies have the political will to deter Soviet moves in Asia or Africa by the threat of a response in Europe. Mr. Schmidt's approach does not say an emphatic "no" to this reasoning, but the Chancellor certainly would prefer to avoid the issue.

Why the Soviet Union by its sudden announcement of planned partial troop withdrawals from Afghanistan actually provoked the West to close ranks at Venice was analyzed by Flora Lewis in "Summitry Creeps Higher" (6/24/80). Reston then argued "In Defense of Summits" (6/25/80), while on the same date R. W. Apple warned that "In the Rosy Afterglow of Venice Parley, Divisions Remain."

After the Venice summit, the topic of general relations between the United States and the EEC distinctly receded in *The New York Times*. There were two pieces by Paul Lewis in "The Week in Review" (6/29/80) that touched upon the problems of fuel strategy and the perennial agricultural troubles that weaken the basis of the EEC.

NATO, Arms Control Issues, and European Strategy

The core of the Atlantic relationship remains the military security of the area. *The New York Times* has several first-rate experts in security and arms control matters. During the period of reference, 35 stories related to these topics appeared. Six of them started on the front page. The reader got a fair description of both American and European attitudes toward the state of the alliance in the aftermath of the Soviet occupation of Afghanistan. There is no doubt that such *New York Times'* reporters as Drew Middleton, Richard Burt, Flora Lewis, and Bernard Gwertzman have excellent access to their sources in the defense ministries, the foreign offices, and the intelligence agencies in Washington, Paris, London, Bonn, and at SHAPE in Casteau.

The careful reader could find out the subtle differences of approach to strategic matters among the National Security Council, the Pentagon, and the State Department in the United States, NATO officials and other national defense, security and arms control experts. Burt, for instance, was closely informed by the president's national security advisor. Whatever he wrote could be taken as an accurate reflection of current strategic thinking and planning by the National Security Council (NSC), its chief, or his aides. It often appeared as if Burt were used to transmit messages or feelings by the NSC staff to the allies. Thus, "officials"—the invariable description of nonattributable sources in Washington—were apt to tell Burt what they proposed to say in meetings with allies or even to use his stories as trial balloons. Nowhere else in the paper could the time-honored practice of this art, which the late John Foster Dulles brought to perfection, be seen so clearly. Thus, Burt reported on plans for the alliance being pressed at the highest Washington level (4/14/80), on a shift of the U.S. strategy focus from Europe to the Pacific (5/25/80), on the concerns over Chancellor Schmidt's trip to Moscow and its impact on the plan for theater-weapon modernization in NATO (7/2/80), and on Pentagon efforts to reassure the allies about the "countervailing" nuclear strategy as contained in Presidential Directive 59. Here are samples:

> While acknowledging . . . difficulties, a ranking Government official said today that the Administration expected NATO governments to go along with its plan. "If the Europeans can't strengthen themselves in Europe while we carry the can for them in the Persian Gulf," the official said, "then I'm really worried about the future of the alliance." [4/14/80]

> President Carter agreed last month to a new strategic plan that no longer commits Washington to send Pacific-based forces to Europe in the event of Soviet attack there, according to Government officials. . . .
> Discussing the option to use the forces in Europe if necessary, a senior Pentagon official said: "We now have more flexibility to determine if and when this would be necessary. We may have to keep our forces in the Pacific, move them into the Indian Ocean or send them to Western Europe. It will depend on the circumstances." [5/25/80]

> Although Mr. Schmidt is viewed as a strong supporter of continued security ties with Washington, some State Department aides believe that his party is swinging toward the left and under extraordinary circumstances could conceivably favor leaving the Western alliance at a future date. [7/2/80]

Flora Lewis characterized the mood in NATO as one of improved but still uncertain solidarity on the Afghan crisis (5/15/80). She also analyzed the impact of the Soviet "peace-offensive" on Western Europe (5/23/80), the prospects for arms control (6/27/80 and 7/4/80), and finally the effects of the new nuclear strategy (8/15/80). As in other fields, her analyses were thorough, with a responsible weighing of the pros and cons, based upon wide historical and personal knowledge and a true feeling for European thought. Some excerpts:

> The surface of Atlantic relations has been soothed a little on the surface, but the waters below remain roiled. The attempt to convince the Russians that they must reckon with a firmly united and resistant West has not yet become anything like demonstrably persuasive. [5/15/80]

> Western Europe is being told with growing insistence by the Russians that the Soviet presence in Afghanistan is no threat to Europe but that peace is endangered by American policy. . . .
> Those who criticize the Western European governments for hesitating to rebuff Moscow have been speaking of a modern Munich, or a futile effort to preserve peace through appeasement, and even of Vichy, the symbol of active collaboration with an invading power in hopes of mitigating its wrath. [5/23/80]

> Bouncing back to business as usual would certainly convince Moscow that its Afghan venture was paying off. Refusing to proceed with arms control efforts would not only remove Soviet incentive to restraint, it would doom the U.S. to unlimited arms spending which the allies are unlikely to support. [7/4/80]

Drew Middleton, the military expert of *The New York Times*, always tries to present a blend between current American thinking and the views of NATO experts from the European countries. He focused his reports on threats from areas external to NATO proper, a topic imposed by developments in Iran and Afghanistan. He wrote about Soviet worries concerning China, as seen from SHAPE:

> The consensus at headquarters here is that, if the Russians were sufficiently worried by the prospect of a Chinese-American alliance, they could attack and take Manchuria, which produces half of China's oil and a third of its steel. [5/22/80]

He reported allied doubts concerning America's strength in a crisis:

> The general criticism among officials, especially those connected with intelligence, and among military officers is that the United States has failed to grasp the consequences to international stability of the steady expansion of Soviet nuclear and conventional military power. [6/9/80]

He pointed out the military's anxiety over threats of war outside Europe:

> Most NATO military men appear convinced that the present leadership of the Soviet Union would not embark on military adventures that carry the danger of nuclear war. But they add that what they see as a slight Soviet

advantage in strategic nuclear weapons suggests that conventional operations could be launched with impunity against targets of opportunity in the
third world. As matters stand the mission of meeting such operations
would be left to the Americans, British and French. [6/29/80]

And he drew attention to the fact that the Greek-Turkish feud sapped
power from the Eastern flank of NATO (6/2/80).

John Vinocur, the Bonn correspondent, wrote an informative piece
about the expected effects of the lifting of hitherto existing curbs on the
size of the West German fleet (7/18/80). The ongoing discussion of the
necessity to protect NATO's northern flank was the basis for reports by
R. W. Apple from Norway (8/14/80) and Denmark (8/29/80).

Relations with the Federal Republic

The Federal Republic of Germany is, within NATO, commonly referred
to as the most important ally of the United States. Since the tenures of
Drew Middleton and of Clifton Daniel, *The New York Times'* correspondents in Bonn have always been very critical observers of the German
scene. Their memories of the Third Reich and the Second World War
have been mixed with a justifiable pride in the decisive American influence upon the creation of a new, democratic West German state. This
they have followed up by constant and penetrating observations of the
economic, political, and military growth of the erstwhile "pupil."

The present Bonn correspondent of *The New York Times*, John Vinocur,
is no exception to that rule. Ever since his assignment to West Germany,
he seems to have been bent upon finding vestiges of the Nazi past or
fault with the new German political power as personified by Chancellor
Helmut Schmidt.

The FRG's 1980 election campaign (which had four more weeks to go
when this review was submitted) was, as far as analysis goes, not a
front-page matter for *The New York Times*. Vinocur wrote, however, three
analytical pieces about it. On 4/14/80, he described quite pertinently the
clash of ideas and personalities between Schmidt and Franz-Josef
Strauss, his Christian-Democratic opponent:

> Mr. Schmidt has publicly recognized that Mr. Strauss, long pictured as a
> cold warrior and conservative bogeyman, is trying to behave in a states-
> manlike way. But he has been quick to stress that Mr. Strauss is an incalcu-
> lable element. The Bavarian Premier only appears to be decisive, Mr.
> Schmidt says, but in reality delays decisions until his back is against the
> wall. "Where he goes off," the Chancellor said, "is in not being able to hold
> onto cool reason in the most difficult situations."
>
> Returning the personality volley, Mr. Strauss often refers to Mr. Schmidt

as "a dwarf in a hero outfit." Rather than being an incisive manager of state affairs, Mr. Schmidt is in fact a hostage of the left wing of his party, Mr. Strauss says.

On 5/23/80, Vinocur wrote an account of Volker Schloendorff's "unashamedly polemical" film about Strauss ("Der Kandidat"):

> The portrayal of Mr. Strauss as a danger to the existence of West Germany suggests [a problem] in a country with a short democratic history.
> [It] is that characterizing as an evil force a man who even left-wing members of the Social Democratic Party insist is not a fascist seems to betray a kind of insecurity about the democratic process itself, a need for polemics and bogeymen of a kind that have deep roots in German history.

On 7/25/80, he characterized the German election campaign in "Schmidt vs. Strauss: They're Using Bare Knuckles":

> But Mr. Strauss's Bavarian-based Christian Social Union has engaged in its share of mudslinging, attacking Chancellor Helmut Schmidt in a campaign film called "The End of a Legend.". . .
> The "You're-an-old-Nazi-or-an-old-Communist" accusations can still cause a stir in West German politics. In the past both sides have generally appeared to want to avoid skirmishing in this area, sensing their potential vulnerability. But recent exchanges suggested that restraints are gone. . . .
> Mr. Schmidt, the film asserted, is an accomplished actor who has mastered the role of the upright citizen. But the sound track urged voters to examine who his most aggressive publicists are. It listed them as Rudolf Augstein, the publisher of the news magazine Der Spiegel, who it said had been arrested for the possession of narcotics but failed to mention that the charges were eventually dropped; Henri Nannen, chief editor of Stern, a weekly magazine, who was shown wearing a Nazi uniform and described as a former Nazi propagandist, and Mr. Engelmann, who the film said passed bad checks.

One of the most sensitive aspects of the American-German relationship was the validity and relative strength of the political and military ties between Washington and Bonn, and, in a personal realm, the way President Carter and Chancellor Schmidt regarded each other. This was, of course, a matter of fascination for *The New York Times'* correspondent in Bonn. Vinocur tried to trace as many parts of this picture as possible. On 4/18/80, he noted in a short story that Günter Grass (author of *The Tin Drum*, among other works) had urged Schmidt to shun the United States in the matter of the boycott of the Moscow Olympics and, in general, to move away from the United States. He then described (in "The Week in Review," 5/11/80) how the chancellor cracked down on this and other signs of "creeping anti-Americanism in his party":

Mr. Schmidt's reaction showed that he thought Mr. Grass was wading toward some wild, uncharted shores that were better left unexplored. Through his press spokesman and then in a personal meeting, the Chancellor reached out and pulled Mr. Grass back. In tones not ordinarily used for dealing with such a national intellectual institution, especially one who has been a Social Democratic speechwriter, the novelist's letter was described as unacceptable, unbalanced and missing the point that the Americans were reacting to situations in Afghanistan and Iran that they didn't create. Forgotten for the moment was whether American policy was prudent or realistic; the letter, Mr. Grass was told, could be seen as the start of an intellectual open season on the United States, and therefore, was dangerous. . . .

The exercise seemed to demonstrate that Mr. Schmidt, when deeply concerned, can push the left wing of his party into line, a task that the opposition maintains he has been scared to do.

His most pertinent analysis of what was, in many quarters, perceived as the distinct cooling off of German feelings toward the United States was written on 6/4/80, based partly on his reading of the German press:

Two unusual articles on the subject appeared recently in Die Zeit, the Hamburg weekly newspaper that probably has a greater following in the West German intellectual community than any other publication. Gerd Bucerius, the newspaper's principal shareholder, wrote in a commentary in the current issue that Mr. [Hans-Dietrich] Genscher thought he might win votes for his party by showing strong support for the United States in connection with the world crises.

"Genscher was wrong," Mr. Bucerius said. "The Germans are eager to be left out of international conflicts. They are, of course, for loyalty, but when they say 'loyalty,' they mean above all American loyalty to Europe. Somehow in the last months the conviction has grown that in an emergency the Federal Republic could get along without the Americans—and under some circumstances do even better."

Another article in the same newspaper by Klaus Harpprecht, who for years served as a speechwriter for Willy Brandt, delved deeply into what he described as the prevalent mood among opinion makers in the country, particularly among the materially comfortable intellectual upper class.

"The key word America brings scorn to people's eyes and they purse their lips," Mr. Harpprecht wrote describing the mood at a fashionable Hamburg party.

The sources for that article seemed to have been chosen in such a way as to prove the point and to make it appear that the anti-American undercurrent had seized most West Germans. Thus, despite Vinocur's report in the same article of a public opinion poll showing that 55 percent of West Germans still regarded the United States as their "best friend," the reader could come away with the impression that the "big brother" relationship between America and Germany "that grew up after World War II" was coming to an end. On the other hand, the insight of his final sentence was well worth noting:

> What the Chancellor has not said is how much he regards the United States' problems as ones of historical disintegration or management that he considers less competent than his own.

Flora Lewis (6/17/80) devoted her column to a conversation with Foreign Minister Genscher. She sympathetically described his efforts to put things into perspective before the summit meeting at Venice:

> In Genscher's view, the principles on which strategic cooperation must be based are clear: the underlying common values and overriding common interests shared by the Western nations. He doesn't like the word "solidarity," which has come into vogue as the panacea for American-European ills, because it implies Europeans are sacrificing or subordinating their own interests to those of the United States. . . .
>
> There is still a revulsion in Bonn against participating in any Western military efforts outside its borders, and this is wise for historical reasons as well as useful for the emphasis it gives to the economic aspect of Western security, too often underestimated in the U.S. It isn't just arms that will help Pakistan, for example, resist tremendous Soviet pressures, but aid to meet the risk of destabilization inherent in a very wobbly economy having to accommodate three-quarters of a million Afghan refugees. Bonn is contributing.

Just prior to the Venice meeting came one of the often-cited "flaps" in the relationship: the leaking of the contents of Carter's strongly worded letter to Schmidt about a reported plan by the chancellor to "freeze" the NATO decision to put new medium-range strategic weapons into Western Europe. Again, Flora Lewis (6/20/80) tried to defuse what seemed to be a new contre-temps between the president and the chancellor:

> When John F. Kennedy was President, wags said that he automatically picked up a special phone which rang on his desk each day and said, "Yes, Chancellor Adenauer, we still love you and support West Germany." He didn't stop to ask who was calling. Bonn's yearning for reassurance was insatiable.
>
> Now, the same phone line seems to be needed, in the opposite direction. There is no evidence of weakening in Chancellor Helmut Schmidt's dedication to the Atlantic alliance or in his determination to deploy medium-range American missiles, unless Moscow makes real concessions on its missile program.

At Venice, Schmidt, apparently unwilling to accord such a favor to the resident *New York Times'* correspondent in Bonn, explained his strategy for forthcoming talks with Soviet President Brezhnev to James Reston (6/24/80). The contents of the German-Soviet summit were correctly and objectively reported by the then *New York Times'* correspondent in Moscow, Craig R. Whitney, who had been Vinocur's predecessor in Bonn. Richard Burt, the strategic specialist of *The New York Times'* Washington office, who could generally be counted on to reflect the attitudes of Dr. Zbigniew Brzezinski, President Carter's national security advisor (or of his staff, many of whom seemed to cultivate an ingrained skepticism toward Germany), was the first to report that the Soviets, in their talks with Schmidt, seemed to have dropped the demand that the West abandon the modernization of its theater nuclear forces as a precondition for future arms-control talks. An analysis of the state of the American-German relationship was contributed (7/4/80) by David Binder, also a former Bonn correspondent who, during his tenure, had very close ties to then Chancellor Willy Brandt and to the Social Democratic leadership. While his article was headlined "Bumpy Marriage Endures," he went to the heart of "the divergency of views between Bonn and Washington on the central issue of how to deal with the Soviet Union":

> For Washington, particularly under President Carter, the relationship with Moscow has been treated almost as a faucet that could be turned off or on. For Bonn, in the decade of its treaty ties, the relationship with Moscow has become a permanent aspect of its foreign relations, augmented by sizable trade and other exchanges, including the repatriation of hundreds of thousands of ethnic Germans from Eastern Europe.

There was not much reporting about the relationship between the two German states. On 7/20/80, a story was filed from Herleshausen on how the two Germanies "move closer, but not along the border," pointing out that the German Democratic Republic (East Germany) has, ever since the early 1970s and the establishment of official relations with Bonn, considerably reinforced its fortifications along the border. Vinocur reported (8/23/80) that Schmidt, in view of the events in Poland, had cancelled what was to have been the first visit by a West German head of government to East Germany in ten years:

> Mr. Schmidt had seemed to be in a no-win situation. If he took the trip and violence developed in Poland while he was the guest of Erich Honecker, the East German leader, he could be accused of lacking political foresight. If the trip ended without significant change in the situation in Poland, he could be accused of betraying the interests of the Polish workers by meeting with a hard-line Communist while their strike continued.

This was highly important news. It made page one in the same day's *Washington Post* and *Baltimore Sun,* which had reports by their own Bonn correspondents. But it rated page six in *The New York Times.* In "The Week in Review" (8/24/80), however, there appeared an analysis by Vinocur, "Ostpolitik Becomes Impolitic for Now," in which he wrote:

> It was going to be Helmut Schmidt's Ostpolitik fortnight, two weeks of talk (and pre-election television prime time) that the West German leader hoped would provide enough East-West good news and momentum to push Afghanistan into an even more forgotten corner. It didn't work out that way.
>
> Busy with strikes at home that were fast making him a figure of diminished influence internationally, Edward Gierek, the Polish Communist leader, decided he couldn't come to Mr. Schmidt's little house in Hamburg last week as planned. . . .
>
> The Gierek no-show left Mr. Schmidt with his visit to East Germany, a trip that once seemed the perfect pre-election show of statesmanship and humanity, but suddenly was transformed by the events in Poland into a difficult, unpredictable and thus politically risky assignment. . . .
>
> The fact was, the trip had become so laden with potential trouble for the Chancellor—photos of him enjoying East German hospitality while Polish workers clung desperately to their goals—that the no-go decision was pure political logic.

The intent here was clearly to show Schmidt as someone who works, if it suits him, against Washington's wishes, who refuses to go along, and whose hand was forced only by the turn of events in Poland.

Vinocur is a gifted feature writer. He uses this talent both in Bonn and during his frequent trips within central and northern Europe. Two examples during this period were: "Visit Tests Emotions of Jews Driven from Germany" (5/31/80) and "Hitler's Alpine Hideaway Is a Tourist Town's Gold Mine" (8/24/80):

> Last week Walter Speyer walked into the street here where the Gestapo arrested him in 1938. . . .

> Each year 275,000 tourists visit the Obersalzberg, a plateau three miles east of this Alpine town on the Austrian border. Here Hitler built the Berghof, an extravagant art-filled retreat, and was soon joined by Goebbels, Göring, Bormann and platoons of lesser Nazi Party officials. . . .

It seemed to this reviewer that both stories reflected Vinocur's feelings toward Germany: a constant, nagging doubt as to whether today's Germans have really overcome a sordid past. He thus plants doubts in his readers' mind, which, one surmises, would only tend to confirm a skepticism toward Germany that still prevails in parts of America's liberal and intellectual establishment.

Relations with the Soviet Union

Although newspaper coverage of the relationship between the two
superpowers merits a special study, a few remarks about *The New York
Times'* coverage of the Soviet Union are included here for the simple
reason that U.S.–European relations cannot be disassociated from the
currents between Washington and Moscow. This period covers, after all,
a time during which, owing to the invasion of Afghanistan, relations in
the West were considerably affected by the heightened tensions between
the United States and the USSR.

Craig Whitney, then *The New York Times'* bureau chief in Moscow,
wrote an excellent analysis of Soviet aims after Secretary of State
Muskie's first encounter with Foreign Minister Gromyko in Vienna
("The Week in Review," 5/18/80):

> [I]t is hard to see how there can be any improvement [in U.S.–Soviet
> relations], no matter who is Secretary of State. All the anti-Brzezinski cari-
> catures flooding the Soviet press, all the advance promotion of Mr. Muskie
> as a counterweight, are really aimed at keeping Soviet readers convinced
> that the Kremlin is not to blame for the tensions. Given the growing insecu-
> rity in the United States about American military strength, given the will-
> ingness to use theirs that the Russians are demonstrating in Afghanistan,
> there can be little doubt that no matter who is President during the next
> four years, Soviet-American detente, as the early 1970's knew it, is dead.
> Meanwhile, Moscow is trying to drive wedges between Washington and its
> allies in Europe and Asia, to convince them that their interests lie in sepa-
> rate relationships with Moscow.

It had become evident that the stalemate in the dialogue between the
United States and the Soviet Union would last for quite some time,
especially vis-à-vis the presidential election. After that, apart from some
color stories about Moscow and Leningrad in view of the forthcoming
Olympic Games, it took several weeks until Leslie Gelb, a former *New
York Times* man and former director of the State Department's Bureau of
Politico-Military Affairs, tried to analyze the findings of his visit to
Moscow from a strategic angle (7/9/80):

> Just as Richard M. Nixon tried to get out of a similar dilemma in Vietnam
> [i.e., similar to the Soviet dilemma in Afghanistan] by going to Moscow,
> Moscow is now looking for help from Washington. In the early 1970's,
> President Nixon sought Moscow's aid in putting pressure on Hanoi to slow
> down the war against South Vietnam in return for which Washington
> would agree to establish detente. Now, Moscow is seeking Washington's

help in tamping down military support for the Afghan guerrillas in return for which Moscow would be willing to re-establish detente. The reasoning is simple: Without detente, everything becomes more costly and more dangerous for Moscow and the West. This time, the only hitch is that Washington is not making this calculation the same way.

Flora Lewis followed with columns from Moscow and Kiev (7/22/80, 7/25/80, 7/29/80), giving her own analysis of Soviet attitudes:

[A] senior Soviet editor, who said he understood the United States well, added that some "details" still baffled him. "For example," he said, "I don't see why you boycotted the Olympics." For him, Afghanistan is a local matter that shouldn't concern Americans any more than he claimed Russians would mind "if you needed some security measures on your Mexican border." [7/25/80]

After the "new" American nuclear strategy—the shift to the "countervailing force concept"—was made public by leaks from Presidential Directive 59, Soviet reactions became of interest. Anthony Austin, Whitney's successor in Moscow, wrote five stories about that topic. The most important (8/25/80) was based on that very rare occasion, a direct interview with a ranking Soviet official, in this case, Lieutenant General Mikhail Milshtein, a political-military advisor to the Institute of the United States and Canada:

Q. How do you evaluate the shift in American nuclear targeting policy?. . .
A. What is new now, it seems to me, is that the possibility of waging nuclear war has been accepted on the very highest levels of the American Government. The acceptability of nuclear war. And the possibility of victory in such a war.

After that, quite naturally, Austin's main focus became the Soviet attitude toward the Polish workers' strikes in August. None of his reports on this subject, except a story on 8/21/80 about the resumption of jamming of certain Western broadcasts during the Polish crisis, was published on page one. It seems to this reviewer that, again, there might have been a conscious decision at the editorial level of *The New York Times* in New York to conform with the Carter administration's deliberate "low profile" vis-à-vis the USSR by relegating news from Moscow to rather subordinate spaces. The question here is not whether one "likes" the USSR or, indeed, opposes its system, but one of relativity of forces, especially in the context of the U.S.–European relationship.

Relations with Eastern Europe

There was a stark contrast to the reporting from Moscow: *The New York Times* definitely excelled during the whole period of reference in its coverage of Eastern Europe. In both quality and quantity, this surpassed its coverage of Western Europe in many respects. Was this also the result of a conscious decision at the paper's headquarters in the sense that Washington's official policy, after Afghanistan, differentiated purposely between Moscow and the Eastern European countries? Apart from the event-prone reporting about President Tito's death and funeral and connected political speculations, the bulk of reporting out of Eastern Europe came, even before the workers' strikes on Poland's Baltic coast in August, from Poland generally.

John Darnton, *The New York Times'* correspondent in Poland, did a brilliant job in describing the domestic and international effects of the upsets that occurred once more in that crucial hinge between the USSR and the rest of Europe. The readers of *The New York Times* could, indeed, not only follow the day-to-day events at the Lenin shipyards at Gdansk and the agonizing reappraisals of the party leadership in Warsaw, but also find in-depth analyses of the historical and immediate reasons for the third Polish unrest in 24 years. Flora Lewis, during her visits to Warsaw (7/15/80 and 7/18/80) and to Prague (8/5/80 and 8/8/80), sensed the tide of things to come, and in her analysis in "The Week in Review" (7/27/80) foresaw the impact of the strikes:

> So the confrontation, peaceable so far, between workers and state around the country is in fact a crisis in the regime and everybody knows it. At the same time, practically everybody knows that violent upheaval would be a catastrophe for Poland. Nobody wants Soviet tanks in the street, and Moscow doesn't want to be faced with a Polish insurrection.
>
> The impasse is producing some astonishing results. The regime still pretends to be the vanguard of the working class, but officials argue about how much they have to give, tacitly admitting that they are bosses haggling with legitimate labor claims. The workers have formed delegations that negotiate with managers, something unheard of in the Soviet bloc, and possibly the embryo of real unions.

The fundamental contrast to the "Prague Spring" of 1968 was that the Soviet Union did not immediately intervene with its military forces in Poland. Given almost totally unhindered Western media coverage of the Gdansk strikes, Poland was opened to outside view much as Czechoslovakia was prior to the Soviet reoccupation there. In both cases sudden crisis in an Eastern socialist country produced a concentrated flow of foreign reporting back to the West. Adding to the drama of the events themselves, no doubt, was the convergence of other facts and feelings: the strategic position of Poland on the map of Europe, the deep-rooted sympathetic sentiments in the West (one need only mention the twelve million Polish-Americans), and the importance of a Pole as Pope of the Roman Catholic Church. John Darnton's analysis in "The Week in Review" (8/24/80) was as vivid as it was insightful:

> The root of discontent is economic, and without the country's awesome, perhaps insolvable, economic problems, other grievances would probably never surface. Meat is the evocative symbol. When it is not available, all the other sacrifices endured in the name of building socialism seem that much more unbearable. Since 1971, the policy of party leader Edward Gierek has been a crash program to raise living standards. The country's late great poet, Antoni Slonimski, called it "stuffing their mouth with sausage so they'll shut up." The problem with material benefits purchasing loyalty is that it can backfire: When the sausage is gone, there is no other reason to support the Government.

Flora Lewis (8/28/80) related Poland's plight to the rest of Eastern Europe:

> There is some paradox in comparison of the Hungarian and Polish situations. The Hungarian revolution was sparked by upheavals in Poland in 1956, when it appeared that the Poles won and the Hungarians lost. But later the substantial liberalization obtained by the Poles was rapidly eroded and repression restored in many fields, while the Hungarians quietly and gradually won concessions. It is undoubtedly the memory of the disillusionment after what seemed like victory in 1956 and again in 1970, when Edward Gierek came to power, that makes the Polish workers so distrustful of the current Government's promises.

Poland was also the subject of *New York Times* editorials, which otherwise gave sparse attention to European affairs.

Relations with the United Kingdom

The extent of change and emphasis in U.S.–European relations could also be seen in *The New York Times'* coverage of events in the United Kingdom. They rated only six stories on page one, three of which were related to the successful storming of the Iranian Embassy in London by British commandos, one to the country's economic problems, and another (from Washington) to the intended purchase of American "Trident" missiles by the British armed forces. If one remembers the preeminence of news from the United Kingdom during the postwar years and well into the 1960s, its relative scarcity during this period suggested an erosion of what was once called the "special relationship" between the two Anglo-Saxon countries. Before the Venice summit, R. W. Apple, *The New York Times'* correspondent in London, lucidly explained Prime Minister Thatcher's difficulties in trying to become a sort of go-between agent ("The Week in Review," 6/8/80):

> British policy has . . . tended to be ambiguous, resting in recent years on the idea that, by joining Europe, Britain could act as honest broker between the Common Market and the United States.
> Lately, that hasn't worked well. Britain tried to act as the American friend at court on Afghanistan and Iran, foreign policy questions about which Mr. Carter cares deeply. Mrs. Thatcher called early and strongly for a boycott of the Olympic Games in Moscow. Lord Carrington, her Foreign Secretary, took the lead in attempting to sell the Continental countries on economic sanctions against Teheran.
> But the British Olympic Committee paid the Prime Minister no heed, voting to send a team to Moscow over Government objections. That made Mrs. Thatcher look foolish at home. It irritated West Germany, which worked quietly and successfully in support of the boycott, and the French Government, which tried to do the same thing and contends it might have succeeded had Mrs. Thatcher not failed. Washington was also displeased.

Flora Lewis described how "Some Economic Cures Can Kill" (7/9/80). Apple noted (7/23/80) that Britain's jobless rate had reached its highest level since the 1930s. He also described internal dissensions within the Labour Party (8/4/80). William Borders (8/24/80) gave a vivid description of the effects of recession upon a family's way of life. But it was left to an Englishman, Harold Jackson, the *Guardian's* chief correspondent in the United States, to analyze in a guest column (8/27/80) the question, why "Britain Isn't Europe":

> Think about it. While we have passed the centuries surrounded by all that lovely water, the Europeans have passed their time overrunning one another's territory, disrupting orderly government and generally failing to sort themselves out. The Germans and the Italians didn't even achieve entity until 800 years after we did, and the Belgians still can't get their act together.
> Only the Icelanders, also an island nation, got around to parliamentary government before we did and that fact is deeply relevant to our view of Europe. The evolution of the Common Market is firmly embedded in the European tradition—long on bureaucracy and short on democracy.

The reporting from the United Kingdom was definitely "low key." Did that reflect the relative interest that events in Britain provoke these days in the United States?

Relations with France

Undeniably, the relationship of the United States with France has always been—and, so this reviewer trusts in spite of the many mutual irritations ever since the end of the Second World War, always will be—a truly special chapter. In it, one sees the ups and downs of friendship mixed with condescension on the part of the French, and the historic desire to be loved and understood, mixed with genuine shocks and frustration, on the part of the Americans. Reports from *New York Times'* correspondents in France were far more numerous—over 50—than from either the Federal Republic or from the United Kingdom, although they appeared only four times on page one. As always, France provoked not only the political, but also the literary and human interest of the observer.

The reasons for President Giscard d'Estaing's meeting with Soviet President Brezhnev at Warsaw and for France's insistence upon planning and executing its national foreign policy without prior consultation even with its closest allies were explained by Paul Lewis (5/22/80):

> On the dispute over the French-Soviet meeting, Mr. François-Poncet recalled in the French Parliament that Mr. Muskie had described his own talks with Foreign Minister Andrei A. Gromyko in Vienna as "useful and necessary."
>
> "How can something judged useful and necessary when it involves Mr. Muskie and Mr. Gromyko become damaging and unnecessary when the French President and Mr. Brezhnev are concerned?" the French minister said. . . .
>
> In a news conference yesterday, Mr. Muskie indicated his personal irritation over not having been told about the plans when he met with Mr. François-Poncet in Vienna on Friday, three days before the Warsaw session. . . .
>
> If the United States found the three-day notice too short, Mr. François-Poncet said, it has only itself to blame, implying that the State Department could not keep secrets and might have disclosed the plan in a way that would embarrass France.

Flora Lewis, whose base is Paris, gave an excellent description of Giscard's diplomacy in "The Week in Review" (5/25/80):

> [Mr. Giscard d'Estaing] does appreciate the political effect of drama and the

political importance of myth. France's Fifth Republic was, after all, founded by coup d'état, on the myth of superior legitimacy. It was nourished by the myth that prestige and self-assertion implied, indeed created, power. It was consoled by the myth that France could go it alone in the world proclaiming itself leader of all who chafe under the heavy-handedness of superpowers. . . .

The myths are still there. But deep down, people tend to realize they are myths which may not serve against the pitiless force of the harshest realities. Europeans are getting frightened now, the French too. The question they are arguing, without quite facing, is whether the magic of the myths will chase danger away or whether it will have to be confronted. In an intricate way meant both to give solace and to fire determination, Mr. Giscard d'Estaing is answering yes to both sides.

But by far the most explicit piece about France's diplomatic *raison d'être* was a guest column by Michel Jobert, the former foreign minister (5/28/80), in which he repeated his theory and conviction that often irritated Washington during his tenure at the Quai d'Orsay that America's real allies were those who spoke their minds and did not hesitate to differ from Washington when this suited their national interest:

The United States should not be surprised that it now faces vague and reluctant allies. For years, the United States has decided *for* them, not *with* them. It has constantly sought their acceptance of its decisions, not their advice, by means of persuasion or pressure. It has tried to deal with them one by one, because that was easier, rather than promoting their unity, which was difficult but would have been significant for the idea of freedom. On the contrary, the United States encouraged their feeling of dependence, as though Europe's destiny were to bear the burden of both Soviet and American tutelage.

Flora Lewis (6/6/80) analyzed the relationship of new arms and "détente" for France:

Quite simply, the threat of nuclear holocaust may so far have prevented war in Europe, but an all-or-nothing approach to defense is too much to preserve life on earth and too little to preserve the Western way of life.

So France is heading for a broader spectrum of arms as well as more warheads, and a more supple defense doctrine recognizing that it can no more stand alone against the foe than it could in 1940. At the same time, it persists in calling for disarmament and detente. Thumbing nose at the U.S. is a superficial reflex, an irritating habit left over from times when the greatest troubles were internal, not external menace. But rude symbolism is not really policy.

James Reston (6/18/80) talked to Giscard prior to the summit in Venice. In July, it became known that France had successfully tested a neutron warhead. Flora Lewis ("The Week in Review," 7/6/80) analyzed the political and strategic consequences and pointed out which important questions remained unanswered:

> French defense theory assumes that the Russians might try to knock out European-based atomic weapons in a surprise blow, counting on their intercontinental parity to keep Washington from launching long-range missiles. Thus they would dominate the continent without risking Soviet territory. Does France have the means to expand its arsenal to match Soviet advances and counter this risk?
>
> Many French experts and politicians think not. France must reconsider its doctrine, they argue. Some suggest cooperation with Britain, or a European force including Germany, to enlarge the technical-financial base. That would mean ending independence of decision on when to fire and, unless Britain and the continental allies cut their ties to Washington, a return to the Atlantic concept.

When Giscard d'Estaing, during his state visit to West Germany, urged the creation of a "strong and independent Europe," a demand that went to the core of the Atlantic relationship, *The New York Times* ran this as a Reuters story from Bonn on page three.

The development of the French fishermen's strike was good copy and led to a series of stories by Frank Prial and Paul Lewis. The type of color reporting to which Paris has always lent itself was well represented in a notebook report by Richard Eder (7/15/80) that led from Bastille Day observances to politics:

> President Valéry Giscard d'Estaing stood in the reviewing stand with a raincoat but no umbrella. His ministers followed his example. The President's style has been called royal lately; today's watchword seemed to be: "après le déluge, moi." . . . The tendency is to define publicly as problems those things one can make a stab at controlling, and to side-slip the others.
>
> The effect, at least on the outsider, is a simultaneous admiration and exasperation. Ideas and policies may be as polished as the Garde's breast-plates, and as practical as the lights in Paris apartment houses that switch on just long enough to see you up the stairs—assuming you move briskly—and then leave you in darkness. They do, in fact, seem to leave a good deal in darkness.

Eder also wrote a critical analysis (7/27/80) of the dilemma posed by France's close relations with the Arab world: the assassination attempt on former Iranian Prime Minister Bakhtiar once again proved the relative impunity with which hired Arab gunmen seemed to operate in France.

Relations with Southern and Southeastern Europe

Southern and Southeastern Europe are of major importance to the whole of the American-European relationship. The new political regimes in Spain and Portugal and their consequences for the European Community and for NATO, the ongoing struggle between the Christian Democrats, Socialists, and Communists in Italy, the developments in Greece under its new regime with respect to the EEC and NATO and vis-à-vis the Cyprus question and Turkey, and (although Turkey can be seen geographically as part of Asia Minor) the relevance of politics in Ankara to the Atlantic Alliance—all these are of consequence to the United States. This is even more true in view of the proximity of all these countries to the Near East and thus to the problem of energy supplies from the Arab countries to the Western world.

The New York Times published a total of 45 reports from this area during the period of reference: 18 from Italy, nine from Spain and Greece each, five from Turkey, and four from Portugal. Two stories from Italy and one from Spain began on page one.

Henry Tanner, the Rome correspondent of The New York Times, followed closely the ongoing political terrorism and the trials connected with it in Italian courts. He analyzed the deep ideological divisions in the country:

> In a wider sense, it [the case of a Christian Democrat party chief whose son was a suspected terrorist] exposes the labyrinthine complexity of political life in Italy, where not only families but most institutions are torn along party lines. The political parties reach into everything and divide everything. But the lines between them are blurred, because all are part of the establishment. The lines are also blurred by obscure ideological quarrels within the parties, and by personal rivalries, friendships and complicities. The upshot is often Kafkaesque—a world where nothing can be taken for granted and where strange things happen—or fail to happen—in apparent defiance of cause and effect. [6/8/80]

Tanner wrote about the Italian Communists' struggle to hold on to power (6/7/80) and how political balance was maintained in regional elections (6/11/80). The extent of the split that terrorism provoked in Italy was the topic of his analysis ("The Week in Review," 8/17/80) of the aftermath of the bombing at Bologna's main station:

> Not since the days of the kidnap-murder of former Prime Minister Aldo Moro more than two years ago has Italy been so deeply troubled. . . .
> During the Moro affair, there was a consensus among the political parties

about terrorism. Now, however, the communists are in the opposition, driven there by the Christian Democrats' new hard-line leadership, and even the Socialists, who are in the Government coalition, have been attacking the Christian Democrats since Bologna. Rino Formica, a Socialist Cabinet minister, blamed rising terrorism on "Government weakness." The terrorists had found accomplices in the police, a suspicion shared by many Italians. The Interior Minister answered simply that "this is not a time for polemics."

Tanner has always been an excellent observer of violent upheaval: he proved it during the Algerian war and the war in the Congo. He is therefore well suited to analyze the ramifications and the impact of terrorist movements in Italy.

The problems connected with Spain's desire to join the European Economic Community and NATO were the subject of four analyses, two by Jose Antonio Martinez Soler, the chief economic editor of *El Pais,* as a guest columnist ("The Week in Review," 5/11/80 and 5/21/80) and two by James Markham, the *New York Times'* correspondent in Madrid ("The Week in Review," 6/1/80 and 7/27/80). Markham is a thorough and balanced observer. He approaches the story of post-Franco Spain from the political, the economic, and the human angles. He seems to be unprejudiced, which is of essential importance in an area where, owing to long periods of right-wing, Fascist regimes, there is a tendency, especially among liberal Western intellectuals, to measure the results of young democracies against the remnants of old power structures in the political and economic establishment. Markham keeps an eye on the continuing unrest in the Basque region of Spain. He seeks to talk to and discuss problems with intellectuals and representatives of the universities. From all that there emerges an informative picture of today's Spain, although the space given to the topic in the paper is quite small.

Similarly, Markham pointed out the basic political problems Portugal faced as it continued to adjust to the post-Salazar period. He described the struggle between Prime Minister Sa Carneiro and the renewed ambitions of the military, personified by General Soares Carneiro ("The Week in Review," 5/4/80 and 7/21/80). Markham has obviously studied the results of the internal developments in Portugal since 1974 very closely. It is interesting to remember that, during and after the coup against Salazar, *The New York Times* did not have a permanent correspondent in Lisbon. That was when then Secretary of State Kissinger had practically written off Portugal. He was seemingly convinced that the Communists would take over and that Soares' socialists would not be strong enough to thwart a victory by Cunhal. This, fortunately, proved to be an erroneous assumption.

Greece's domestic and international problems did not figure prominently in *The New York Times'* reporting during this period. The change of personalities within the government was summarized by Nicholas Gage, the Athens correspondent (5/15/80). Tensions still existing from the Civil War were his topic on 7/28/80. The two most interesting developments—a move to reintegrate Greece in NATO's military wing and the impact of inflation upon the country's economic boom since 1974— were the subjects of two stories (8/17/80 and 8/24/80). None of these stories appeared on the front page. No analysis was given of the expected impact, both domestically as well as within Europe, of Greece's forthcoming membership in the EEC—a regrettable omission since the political and strategic importance of Greece in the Eastern Mediterranean can hardly be exaggerated.

Two reports by *The New York Times'* correspondent in Ankara showed the extent of the domestic problems besetting Turkey: the probability that new West German visa curbs would severely curtail any further influx of Turkish workers into the Federal Republic (7/25/80), and the rivalry between Prime Minister Demiral and his predecessor Ecevit, particularly its effects on antiterrorist efforts (7/30/80). Apart from a report on the conditions in the Turkish sector of Cyprus and three reports on the trial and verdict against the instigators of the 1978 riots, Turkey did not otherwise appear in the paper's reporting from Southeastern Europe and the Mediterranean area.

Relations with Scandinavia

The New York Times does not have a permanent correspondent in the three Scandinavian countries. The general area of Scandinavia was covered in nine reports, all of which were written by *New York Times'* correspondents from London (R. W. Apple), Bonn (Vinocur), and Paris (Frank Prial). Six related to Sweden, two to Norway, one to Denmark. The industrial strikes in Sweden, which had paralyzed the country in May, were described by Vinocur (5/14/80). Apple reported about the possibility of a Social-Democratic comeback in Sweden (8/20/80). Norway's strategic position on the northern flank of NATO, which had been emphasized in the plans for the alliance's sea strategy for the 1980s, was the subject of a guest column by John C. Ausland, a former American diplomat (5/10/80). The problems and limitations of the social system in Denmark were the topic of an analysis by Prial (8/11/80). None of the reports from Scandinavia appeared on the front page.

Editorials

As noted before, there appeared only 19 editorials in *The New York Times* during this period that related to European questions. This editorial coverage of U.S. –European relations cannot be called dense. This could be explained, perhaps, by the fact that, in contrast to many West European daily newspapers, foreign news in *The New York Times* is presented in five different forms: (1) in correspondents' reports; (2) in their "news analysis" pieces; (3) in signed columns by staff members; (4) in summarized, unsigned "capsules" on the first two pages of "The Week in Review"; (5) and in articles in *The New York Times Magazine*. The "Week in Review" is a special feature for which *The New York Times* merits the envy of many a competitor, even those American newspapers which, like the *Baltimore Sun, The Washington Post,* or *The Washington Star*, publish their own commentary sections on Sundays.

Nevertheless, the political impact of an editorial in *The New York Times* cannot be underestimated. It ought to represent the consensus of its editorial staff on a particular topic and to be understood as their opinion.

The relative scarcity of editorials on European-related questions must be distinguished from their relative quality. And that quality can be, at times, quite remarkable although *The New York Times* rarely engages in the sharp, often subjective polemics that one finds, say, in *The Washington Post*.

On the subject of the alliance and the Venice summit, four editorials were excellent: "The Cracked Alliance" (5/21/80) described in clear, stark terms the main concern underlying the meeting of the chiefs of government—the frailty of the alliance outside of Europe—and came to this rather ominous conclusion:

> Unchecked, the discord will erode the basic military alliance. The purpose of that alliance was to combine European, Japanese and American economic power for the defense of democratic values. What a tragedy if economic interests end up pulling it apart.

In "A Quarrel About More Than Missiles" (6/21/80), one could see an unmistakable message to the leader of a major ally, Chancellor Schmidt. The alliance, it stated, "is in disagreement about the whole East-West relationship." And it castigated Schmidt for his alleged willingness to negotiate a "freeze" upon the deployment of new theater nuclear weapons as had been decided by NATO, warning that the Soviet Union would be the only beneficiary of such a move while also stating that the chancellor's main concern remained the continuation of "détente" in Europe:

> When, in 1977, he was pleading for the missiles he would now risk deferring, Mr. Schmidt expressed concern about Soviet-American parity in nuclear weapons. He said he no longer wanted to rely for his defense only on support from across the ocean. He urged a "Euro-strategic balance" to supplement the global balance. Having cast doubt on the sufficiency of Western arms, he cannot now lightly pretend that all is well or that disagreements exist only in some distant Asian corner.

In "At Sea in Gondolas" (6/22/80), *The New York Times'* lead editorial pointed to the fact that one word described, as it had for six years, the whole preoccupation of the industrial countries with their sanity and, indeed, their survival: oil. The irony in this editorial's last paragraph was one of the best statements one could find in the paper during this whole period:

> Afghanistan? Olympics? Jerusalem and the West Bank? NATO missiles? Aid to Turkey and Pakistan? These issues and Mr. Carter's cry that the Russians are marching will make ironic paragraphs in our grandchildren's history texts, duly illustrated with the faded, sinking splendor of Venice. The leaders of the nations assembled this weekend know, even if they will not say so, that they are headed for an unending series of major oil crises. They will either join together to share the sacrifices and manage the risks, or they will drown in currents that no one will ever believe they could not see.

In "Turkish Anarchy, Western Alarm" (8/15/80), the reader was able to see the grave dangers to Western security that arose because of the internal struggle in a country which, for almost three decades, was seen as one of the main pillars of the alliance.

Four editorials referring to the workers' strikes in Poland must be judged exceptional in their analytical quality: "Demanding the Unthinkable in Poland" (8/19/80) tried to help the American reader to a sense of proportion in the midst of presidential election politics:

> Yet not even in the heat of a political campaign can Americans sanely hope for a violent confrontation between the Gierek regime and the strikers, let alone for Soviet tanks in Poland. Mr. Gierek has shown pragmatic skill in fashioning a Polish model of Communism that affords a measure of national freedom without unduly alarming his Soviet patrons. Americans and Soviets alike have a shared interest in his succeeding again.

The editorial, "What 'Soviet' Means in Poland" (8/24/80), clearly described the impact of the workers' strike on Soviet rulers and their pretense of being the exclusive guardians of pure Marxist-Leninist doctrine:

> The aging Bolsheviks who dominate the Soviet Union have further reason for concern. The strikers in Poland have already formed workers' councils, the embryo of a parallel government, and their demands include, crucially, the right to form independent unions. It's easy to forget that the Russian word for these councils is "soviet." Without Lenin's memorable appeal, "All power to the soviets!" the Bolsheviks might not have prevailed in the October Revolution.
>
> Considering their history, the Poles have good reason to know how Lenin dishonored that promise.

The same editorial acknowledged the limits of possible change:

> What the Baltic workers are doing now . . . is a brave, proud and, alas, probably hopeless gesture. . . . What party chief Edward Gierek would doubtless like to do is yield on bread and butter demands while persuading the insurgents that their political demands ignore compelling "realities."
>
> These realities are plain, and unlovely. . . .
>
> In present circumstances, Washington can do little to help the Polish strikers.

After the settlement at Gdansk, the editorial, "Why the Polish Deal Might Work" (9/3/80), underscored pertinent facts:

> [A] lot has changed since 1956. Poland's workers have been disciplined and restrained; so have their allies among the intellectuals. Poland's pride, and its Catholic Church, have been stiffened by the election of Pope John Paul II. And the Polish economy is vitally dependent on Western governments and bankers. If Moscow overreaches to upset the latest agreements, it risks not just bloodshed but also a financial crisis for both East and West. . . .
>
> American influence in Eastern Europe has been modest for a generation. But the Soviet Union, too, has lost a degree of control. It is in the spaces vacated by the superpowers that Poland's workers may have found new soil for their independence.

Conclusion

It seems to this reviewer that the need for an extended and permanent transatlantic dialogue in the press is as important as ever. Certainly, the

United States has been, for a variety of reasons, more introspective since the mid-1970s. This is commonly explained by the reasons that the double trauma of Vietnam and Watergate had to be overcome, that the nation had to find its inner balance again, that it had to adapt to a fact of life that is difficult for a people who grew up with the belief that there were virtually no limits to American power—that the United States today is no longer the dominating power. That was brought home to America in many ways, strategically as well as economically. It was— and is—not easy to digest. Witness the obvious necessity for presidential candidates to reassure their audiences and voters that, if they are elected or reelected, they will see to it that the United States remains "second to none." This corresponds to the American belief that, once one wants something and the nation puts its hands to the wheels, all problems can be solved. This appeals to simple instincts, to a tendency to see things in black and white where, as President Kennedy already said 18 years ago, there are only "shades of grey." It can, at worst, blind the eye and thus prevent a clear, if often unpleasant, view of the facts.

A newspaper should be not only an opinion maker, a chronologist of current events, but also an educator in the largest sense of this word. Learning about each other, weighing the facts of national priorities against alliance requirements, listening to the other side's argument, especially among friends and allies, are all parts of that process. That, quite often, is not possible because of what former Senator J. William Fulbright once called "the arrogance of power." An aspect of that arrogance is the inclination on the part of Americans to tell the Europeans how to behave, how to adjust to American designs, and, on the European side, a tendency either to teach the Americans in areas where one believes one is ahead of them—or to complain about suffering Washington's neglect.

The New York Times is not absolutely free of such feelings, for it is in many ways a true reflection of what is being thought about Europe in the cosmos of Manhattan or along the East Coast—although, as any observer who cares can find out, "America truly begins West of the Alleghenies."

Maybe meetings, even infrequent ones, between the editors of the most influential newspapers on both sides of the Atlantic, where all these problems can be openly discussed and compared, could significantly contribute to a necessary enlarging of the respective horizons. The need to know seems to have grown proportionally to the shrunken distances of the Atlantic. Certainly, the compelling necessities of our times—political, economic, and strategic, but also human—call for such an intensification of the dialogue.

Response to Reifenberg

Choosing What to Cover

In the weeks immediately following the period spanned by his review, Jan Reifenberg thought that *The New York Times'* coverage of Eastern Europe continued to warrant applause, but called its attention to France "myopic." "While it was understandable because of the natural sympathies of its owners and many of its readers that *The New York Times* would devote so much space to the terrorist bombing in Paris directed against Jews," he said, "other important things happened in France that were not covered." His criticism was again tempered by his praise for Flora Lewis, whose commentary on the bombing was "extraordinarily fair."

Mort Rosenblum, then Editor-in-Chief of the *International Herald Tribune,* protested this line of analysis. "The problem with foreign reporting," he said, "is that it's a cottage industry. What gets reported depends much more on the particular individuals in the field than on any policy, prejudice, or predilection of the newspaper's owners. *The New York Times'* attention to the bombing in Paris owed more to the fact that its correspondent Dick Eder was on the scene than to the religion of the Sulzbergers."

Added Pierre Salinger, Paris Bureau Chief for ABC News, "You can't fault *The New York Times* for its coverage of the Paris bombing when the French press dealt with nothing else!"

Looking again at *The New York Times'* editorials, Reifenberg found the number of them concerned with European affairs "appallingly small—and getting smaller." He went on to say, "Reporting in the U.S. about Europe is ebbing generally. It's non-existent on television. This [general neglect of Europe] may be the larger issue ahead, since, in any case, Reagan's supporters won't grant *The New York Times*—with its predominance of liberal thought—the importance their predecessors did. European correspondents had better get out of Washington and New York to develop a direct awareness of the *other* United States."

In explaining his theory that foreign news coverage in any country tends to diminish as that country's influence in other parts of the world becomes less than it was, Peregrine Worsthorne of the London *Sunday Telegraph* recalled having once been asked to report the exact spellings of the members of a new cabinet in Sudan—an information request that would not even occur, he said, to the editor of a British newspaper today. He did not regret the change, however: "That's an old-fashioned idea—to concentrate on the minutiae of politics. One should instead read books and go for the deeper trends."

Murray Seeger, Brussels correspondent for the *Los Angeles Times*, agreed, but still thought it was "shocking how little the U.S. press covered the middle-sized countries of Europe. England is overcovered, and it goes downhill from there."

Eugene Blabey of United Press International, on the other hand, took issue with the others' perception that American newspapers were de-emphasizing foreign news. He felt they were stepping up such coverage, and he predicted the development in the United States of regional papers and chains that would build their own networks of foreign correspondents.

Dennis Redmont, Rome Bureau Chief for the Associated Press, suggested that government, perhaps more than newspapers themselves, influenced the choice of stories. Coverage in the United States of the Moscow Olympics, for example, fell, he said, because of the government-instigated boycott—as if the U.S. news media were expected to boycott the event no less than the athletes. On a visit back to the States, Redmont "was astonished to find no coverage of the fact that at that time Libya's and Italy's warships were at gunpoint over Malta"—a lapse made explicable, perhaps, only by the fact that the U.S. government itself had not decided to make the incident a matter of its concern. From a wider perspective, Redmont thought that paying less attention to Europe was a factor of making room for "the explosion of reporting now devoted to the Third World."

William Pfaff, who writes from Paris for the *International Herald Tribune* and *The New Yorker*, raised a different question about *The New York Times'* choice of what to cover: "Is this a matter of the editors or a matter of the public? It does seem to me that there was in *The New York Times*, in the days of 'the good, gray *Times*,' dull as it was, interminably telling you again and again the same thing, a certain, austere sense of obligation on the part of editors and publishers: that the *Times* was a newspaper of record; and even if nobody read a story, if it happened, the *Times* would report it. You go to New York now—I was there in February [1980], and a friend who is an editor of *Foreign Affairs* said, 'What is this about Tunisia and Libya? I couldn't find anything in the *Times* about that.' It's my impression that at some point the *Times* decided it had to get more popular or become more accessible, and what happened was a great trivialization."

It was on the heels of that statement that Melvin Lasky, Editor of *Encounter*, asserted: "*The New York Times* now goes for a million readers—its big story is the Big Apple. Reifenberg's critique, far from being critical, is a marvelous example of European generosity. In fact,

The New York Times is so boring, it makes *The Times* of London glisten by comparison. *The New York Times'* top editors are all accomplished and cosmopolitan, so the fact that its stories of the world are so few and far between must stem from their sense of the U.S.'s declining role in the world. They must ask, 'Why do we have to *know* all these details?' and so they don't print them."

Correspondents' Performance

Following the 1980 German election, Reifenberg made a point of proclaiming John Vinocur's coverage of the campaign "outstanding," especially his cover story on Helmut Schmidt in *The New York Times Sunday Magazine.* He also commended Vinocur's account of the East Germans' clampdown at their borders, and its possible long-term effects on East-West relations.

Reifenberg remained bothered, nonetheless, by the way this *New York Times* correspondent in Germany, "like most of his predecessors, seems always to cast a critical eye on everything German." This, Reifenberg compared to the similar tendency of European correspondents, when posted to the United States, "to export their prejudices and, when they arrive, to set out to prove them."

A German government press official echoed Reifenberg's characterization. "Vinocur is good," he said, "but he takes a cold, hard stare, always looking for the SS man around the corner." Of foreign correspondents generally, this official complained, "They're afraid of being indoctrinated. They won't take government statements at face value." He regretted that "most foreign newspapers won't accept our government's support to make it possible for them to send more correspondents abroad." For all that, he admitted that the German press office tends to favor *The New York Times'* correspondent, because of his newspaper's importance, above the others.

Jerome Dumoulin of *L'Express* in Paris defended Vinocur's stance. "Germany is specially sensitive to any suggestion of its being a reluctant ally," said Dumoulin, "but Vinocur is pointing out a tendency, or at least a tension, that is really there. If he's criticized, it's because German leaders somehow *expect* news correspondents to help hold the alliance together."

Günther Gillessen of the *Frankfurter Allgemeine Zeitung* suggested that Germany's foreign correspondents are much freer to choose their stories and thus determine what their newspapers offer than are U.S. correspondents abroad, "who are told how many lines to write and on what." FAZ's correspondents, he said, "are kings in their countries."

That difference, said Friedhelm Kemna, Deputy Editor-in-Chief of *Die Welt* in Bonn, might help to explain the behavior of *The New York Times'* correspondents. The period of Reifenberg's review chanced to reflect relatively well on *The New York Times;* "in other periods, you wouldn't have found a single article. A correspondent like Vinocur is often frustrated; perhaps he is driven to be critical in order to get published. The coverage allowed is inconsistent—it depends so much on the stories in the air."

Confirming the phenomenon from the other side of the press-government divide, Renaud Vignal from the French Foreign Ministry said that he had been popular as a press officer for France in Washington in 1975–77 precisely because France then appeared to the United States as "politically risky." Trouble gets attention.

Competing News Media

Murray Seeger expressed the frustration of journalists for other U.S. newspapers, particularly his own, who feel eclipsed by the attention paid to *The New York Times.* The *Los Angeles Times,* he said, has posted nineteen correspondents abroad and is avidly pursuing a new prominence in foreign reporting, based on "a conscious decision to appeal to a literate readership—as opposed to the old notion of trying to put its newspaper in the hands of every citizen in the L.A. area."

"Why do overseas governments react instead to what appears in *The New York Times?*" asked Pierre Salinger. "Because the White House does." *The New York Times'* and *The Washington Post's* influence on policymakers in Washington may far exceed their influence on the U.S. general public, but because it does, he explained, "foreign governments use those channels to *reach* the U.S. government."

If, on the other hand, one's concern is for the public's understanding, Salinger asserted, "then this discussion is archaic: these four newspapers we have just studied have a miniscule influence on the public in their countries as opposed to television's. That's true of newspapers generally. That's why, when I was Press Secretary to President Kenndy, I started live televised presidential press conferences. Even in regard to foreign affairs, though the available airtime is limited, every U.S. television network has more correspondents abroad than *The New York Times.*"

"But remember," said Mort Rosenblum, "*The New York Times* syndicates to some 400 other newspapers in the U.S. and around the world. Its news budgets," that is, what it decides to treat and with what emphasis, "become the news budgets of those other papers and the news agencies, too. Besides, all correspondents—including those who report for television—tend to refer to *The New York Times* to validate what is or is not a story."

"The story for *The New York Times* and the rest of the press in the years ahead—after a tragic, harrowing year for the U.S., a year that produced a pervasive sense that something had to happen—will be," concluded Reifenberg, "nothing less than how the American people define their role in the world—through the optic of the extreme right or down the broad middle stream they have taken before."

—MR

chapter three

The Times (London): News as Literature

Henri Pierre*

The Times began publication (though under a different name for the first three years) in 1785 under founder John Walter, whose family line of owner-publishers lasted until 1908. In the mid-19th century, under editor John T. Delane, *The Times* grew to be the largest and most influential daily in the world. The ownership of the newspaper has changed hands several times in this century, most recently with the purchase by Rupert Murdoch who is conceded to have saved *The Times,* chronically in deficit since the '60s, from extinction. Its excellence in modern times tracks with its succession of notable editors, especially Sir William Haley from 1952 to 1966, and William Rees-Mogg since 1967.†

The period of reference for this study, April through October 1980, was a testing time for European-American relations, embracing news of Iran, the unfortunate Tabas raid, the Venice summits, events in Poland, the coup in Turkey, the Iraq-Iran conflict, and the electoral campaigns in Germany and in the United States. In this survey of *The Times,* I shall use two approaches: (1) a technical appreciation of the news coverage, September 1–October 10, 1980, and (2) a more general assessment of editorial comment and special articles, April–September 1980.

---

*London Correspondent, *Le Monde*

†John C. Merrill and Harold A. Fisher, *The World's Great Dailies* (New York: Hastings House, 1980), pp. 320–329.

A Technical Appreciation

Overall, I think that the news coverage of *The Times* has been satisfactory in volume, but inadequate and less rewarding in quality. This is an opinion based on my reluctance to accept as sacrosanct the basic rule of Anglo-American journalism, that is, to separate news from commentary. The strict application of this rule fails, I think, to give the background and the context which the average reader, unfamiliar with world problems, needs in order to understand and assimilate the news. This reader should be helped in his efforts to comprehend and assess the information.

The presentation in *The Times* of the news from abroad under the main headings ("Western Europe," "Overseas") certainly makes it easier for the average reader to locate the news, but that is not enough. Also, it should be said, the rule of distinguishing the news from commentary tends to depersonalize the news, particularly the correspondents' stories, which too often are colorless, sometimes tedious, and duplicate the very impersonal news agency stories. What is the point of having special correspondents if their stories are not personalized and, by their nature, not different from the work of news agencies?

Certainly, *The Times* publishes much foreign news and should be credited for the excellence of its foreign reports and the many special articles written by distinguished contributors. In other words, the foreign news "menu" is rich, even too rich for an average reader to assimilate. Perhaps some technical device (a bigger headline or a small introduction, for instance) would help to guide one through the maze of news and to an appreciation of its relative importance. Too often, *The Times* coverage looks like a long accumulation of "raw" news, the volume of which may discourage the reader or force him to an effort for which he is not ready. Even at the risk of infringing the rule against mixing news and comment, an interpretive story, an analysis immediately close to the news, would be of greater value to the reader.

It is regrettable that *The Times* does not use its foreign correspondents (some of them outstanding) more fully in lieu of some outside contributors for its special articles or stories in depth. In any case, *The Times'* correspondents should not be limited to the gathering of news. They should be encouraged to interpret events and give a personal appreciation, as their counterparts on competing newspapers—like *The Guardian* or *The Financial Times*—do.

Another problem was demonstrated twice in September when the editorial writers of *The Times* seemed uncoordinated with the foreign correspondents. On the eve of the military coup in Turkey (9/12/80), *The Times'* leader started out, "If military coups were cyclical, Turkey would be due for one any time now." But, contrary to what one might expect with such an alarm, nothing appeared that day from the Ankara correspondent. On the other hand, in addressing Iran-Iraq relations, the editorial writers may have been oblivious of breaking events. The leader of 9/20/80 began: "Tensions between Iran and Iraq have reached dangerous levels. There is talk of war in the air." This appeared when the Beirut correspondent was writing that Iranian tanks and jets had already been put into battle with Iraq.

Poland. The Times' coverage of Poland was not what could have been expected. No doubt the news analysis was rigorous and the reporting accurate. But *The Times* failed to convey the drama and the tensions. Besides the political problems, there was a human-interest story that deserved impressionistic reporting. That was done by some other British newspapers, not to mention the Continental newspapers. It was also surprising that *The Times'* Warsaw correspondent's news analysis (9/3/80) was overshadowed by the large, disproportionate space devoted to the projected, and then cancelled, visit to Poland of a (British) Trade Union Council delegation. About the consequences for the West, and particularly Poland's economic assistance requirements, *The Times* apparently was satisfied to let Mr. Arrigo Levi, the distinguished Italian guest columnist, deal with those problems.

Turkey. As I emphasized before, *The Times'* Ankara correspondent, like many others, did not predict the coup. Or perhaps, for security reasons, he could not communicate the information he had. On 9/13/80, however, the day after the coup, *The Times* published a remarkable story in depth from Peter Hopkirk and Dennis Taylor. But then, *The Times'* readers had to wait until 9/22/80 to have a background explanation of the coup by Mario Modiano. By comparison with some Continental newspapers (particularly *Le Monde*), *The Times'* coverage fell short.

The Gulf War. Obviously, *The Times'* coverage suffered from the serious handicap of having no correspondent in Teheran. It had to rely on the Beirut correspondent who did his best. But on 9/23/80, the war was on the front page, with a special heading inside. The main story was a collective one, written by the "foreign staff," but the coverage became extensive, involving the foreign correspondents as well as the defense and shipping specialists. Perhaps the stories of Nicholas Hirst, specializing in oil problems, should have been taken out of the economic section to join the front page. But it was only on 9/26/80 that *The Times* had a special envoy on the spot in Basra. Up to that date, *The Times* was impaired by a lack of direct reporting, of "choses vues," especially by comparison with some Continental newspapers that had men in both camps. From then on, *The Times'* coverage of the Gulf War was extensive and of good quality.

Franco-British Relations. Prime Minister Thatcher's visit to Paris, and then to Bordeaux, was reported by no fewer than four correspondents: one in Brussels, one in London, and two in Paris. In spite of this effort, and perhaps for technical reasons only, the coverage, particularly its headlines, was inadequate. It missed, or at least it did not stress, the point which came out clearly from the different tone and substance of Mrs. Thatcher's and Mr. Barre's speeches: that reconciliation was not achieved, and that the two leaders maintained their divergent views about the concept and the functioning of the EEC.

American and German Elections. *The Times'* reporting was very extensive and of good quality. But sometimes it got lost in too many details of relatively little interest for a European reader. More specifically, its coverage of the American campaign was too fragmented. A good round-up once a week, describing the evolution of the campaign, or an elaborate story about the two candidates' views on foreign affairs, or a brilliant piece of reportage would have been appreciated.

In spite of some inadequacies and shortcomings, *The Times* is offering its readers enough material to satisfy their appetite for news. Also, it would be unfair not to mention the exceptional series of articles by Roger Owen on the Middle East, and the special article on Yugoslavia by Charles Douglas-Home published on the day of Mrs. Thatcher's stop in Belgrade. More news analyses of the latter type should be published before the event or coincident with it. They are of great help for those readers, probably the majority, who do not know much or enough about the outside world.

A General Appreciation of Editorial Comment and Special Articles

I shall now concentrate on *The Times'* editorials as well as some of its special articles relating directly or indirectly to European–U.S. relations. As this is obviously a subjective review, I selected the quotations that I thought were of special interest—and in support of my assessment. Nonetheless, in order to allow others to judge for themselves, I have quoted extensively. A selection is in itself a challenge to objectivity, which in any case cannot be absolute. I did my best not to betray the spirit of what was written. Still, I apologize for any unintentional or involuntary distortions.

From looking at the editorials overall, it seems to me that *The Times'* views on European-American relations were on the whole in line with the British government's positions. Let me emphasize that I am in no way questioning *The Times'* independence of mind. The "Thunderer" takes its inspiration, even less any directives, from none but itself. Its criticism of British leaders, Mrs. Thatcher included, was harsh, sometimes extremely harsh. But reviewing these months, I found that the criticisms were directed at the tactics and not at the general line and strategy of British official policy. In this respect, besides its unparalleled quality as a newspaper, *The Times* affords a precious supplementary value to the foreign reader. It gives him an articulate and uninhibited view of the U.K. position regarding transatlantic problems.

Actually, the paramount concern of *The Times* (also shared by the British government) during 1980 seemed to be that Europe should not "lose sight of the essential reality that without the protection of the United States it would have no freedom at all" (7/11/80). Hence the imperative need to reaffirm the Atlantic alliance, in spite of Washington's vacillations and the growing doubts about President Carter's ability to lead.

The main fear of *The Times*, so it seemed, was that Europe might drift into some sort of neutralism or "Finlandization." Europe was therefore urged to expand its role and use to the fullest its diplomatic capacity to hold the faltering American leadership within the context of the alliance.

Apparently, *The Times* always keeps in mind the "essential reality" of Europe's need for American protection. During the Iranian crisis, the newspaper was very critical of President Carter's attitude. The more the president asked from his European allies, the more *The Times* (4/19/80) opposed him:

> President Carter is lurching down a road of his own choosing while his allies run after him trying both to stop him and to appear to support him— and failing on both counts. As a result the whole alliance is drifting into danger. . . .
>
> It now needs to be said still more strongly and openly that President Carter is wrong in his treatment of Iran. . . .
>
> History teaches that economic sanctions seldom, if ever, work, and often rebound on those who impose them. . . .
>
> The time has therefore come for the Europeans to look again at their own tactics. Up to a point it has been sensible to give general verbal and political support to Mr. Carter in the hope of gaining influence over his policies and lessening the bitterness of American opinion. Beyond a certain point it becomes less sensible because it means actually participating in

policies which may be dangerous and damaging in the long-term to the interests of the whole alliance. This point is beginning to approach. When the Foreign Ministers meet in Luxembourg next week they will have to try to define it, though not necessarily in public. They will have to ask themselves whether their undoubted obligation to help the United States requires them to act contrary to their convictions and true interests or whether they should define help as helping to save Mr. Carter from the pressures that are propelling him, perhaps even against his own deeper convictions, in the wrong direction.

But, after the Tabas raid, the number-one priority for *The Times* (4/26/80) was to repair the damage already done to the Western alliance:

The raid failed. It strengthened the Russians, reinforced America's enemies and alarmed her friends in the Middle East, and confused and weakened the alliance. . . .

What now is to be done? The governments of the alliance will continue to give their support to the United States. They will no doubt hope that the President will revert to more cautious politics and that he will carry out his promise in yesterday's television broadcast to use the methods of conciliation and diplomacy. . . .

In their dealings with Iran and with the other Islamic powers, European countries should make two points. The first is not to underrate the United States. The United States is still the greatest economic power in the world and one of the two greatest military powers. . . .

The second point is that the United States is not a threat to the Arab and Islamic culture and the Soviet Union is.

In the same week (4/24/80), *The Times'* attempts to reconcile supporting the United States for the alliance's sake while "helping" the United States by showing it the error of its ways were stretched to a distinction between what European governments should do and what newspapers like *The Times* should do:

The European governments rightly want to maintain and support the alliance, and they should not be criticised for going some way in responding to American requests for help, even though they believe that such help is likely to prove damaging to the interests of the United States. The maintenance of the alliance and the confidence of the alliance is a very major objective of international policy. "My ally, right or wrong" has some merit, but not "let me hand you the pistol you wish to put to your head".

Newspapers have a somewhat different duty and have to try and see and state the truth. The truth, which is widely perceived by experts in Washington, by ordinary Americans, and by all the European Governments, is that the escalation of American policy is not the most likely way of freeing the hostages, given the emotional state of revolutionary opinion in

Iran, but is much the most likely way of spreading and strengthening Soviet power. . . .

If one believes that American policy is in danger of moving in a direction which can only be of enormous assistance to the Soviet Union, and is damaging to the United States and to all free nations, it would be treating Americans as children not to say so.

One got the impression from *The Times'* continual, sometimes tortuous explanations of the rightness of criticizing American policies it thought to be wrong that it felt embarrassed, even guilty, for taking such a position.

Throughout the crisis, *The Times* advocated that Europe play a more important role. But a few days before the EEC Venice summit (6/15/80), it raised the alarm over "signs that Europe may be starting to see its interest as fundamentally different from those of the United States." Now the blame was on the Europeans too eager to save the gains of détente, exposing themselves to blackmail:

[N]either better presidents nor better machinery would have been so missed in recent months if Europe and America had seen their interests in the same terms. The fact that they did not is more worrying than the failures of consultation or the clashes of personality.

Essentially what has happened in recent years is that Europe has acquired a greater stake in European detente than the Americans, as well as a greater stake in Arab oil. . . .

Europeans reacted with an instinctive desire to save the gains of detente in Europe. But once these gains are seen as more valuable to the west than to the east they expose the west to blackmail. It is therefore essential to show readiness to sacrifice them even while trying to save them. This test Europe failed.

This editorial went on to state *The Times'* fundamental conviction:

There is in fact no doubt that a current of opinion in Europe is flowing towards neutralism, "Finlandization" or whatever name is given to a policy of accommodating rather than confronting the Soviet Union. . . . This is a dangerous trend because it could tempt Europe to detach itself from the United States, thereby driving the Americans back into isolationism and diminishing European influence over American policy at a time when it is most needed.

The trend is also dangerous because it derives from too narrow a perception of European interests. Even if over the years western Europe could diminish its reliance on American forces by greater defence spending, it could not significantly lessen its dependence on overseas oil and raw materials and the sea routes which carry them. For a time it might sustain these interests by diplomatic and economic means but they would be very vulnerable unless backed by American military power. To assume that the United States would provide this backing without the structures and obligations of a European alliance is unrealistic. For this reason, if for no other, the long-term interests of Europe and the United States are in fact inextricably bound together, and any European perceptions to the contrary are false.

Who among the European leaders was the best qualified to speak for Europe? *The Times'* answer (6/13/80) was Chancellor Schmidt, whom it had already named in an earlier editorial as the man to explore the possibility of improving the international situation. The chancellor was "a European leader to trust," "one of the strongest and most reliable political leaders in Europe," and this praise contrasted markedly with the editorial remarks on President Giscard d'Estaing:

Herr Schmidt will be going to Moscow at the end of this month as the first western leader to do so since the invasion of Afghanistan. His meeting with Mr. Brezhnev will be very different from President Giscard's furtive and irresponsible meeting with the Soviet leader in Warsaw. That was undertaken without serious preparation, without consultation with France's allies, and without any prospect of results. The President has been deservedly criticized at home. Herr Schmidt, in contrast, is seeking the full backing of his allies and will carry with him their agreed position and their mandate. He will also have the advantage that the Soviet Union takes West Germany extremely seriously as the major power in Europe, whereas on the whole it regards France as useful only for its nuisance value in the western alliance.

The criticism of Giscard, first muted or indirect, expressed itself openly and vigorously in an editorial (7/11/80) in which *The Times* declared itself satisfied that Bonn did not follow the "Pied Piper of Europe." But at the same time, it admitted that domestic political considerations were obliging Giscard to take a public attitude distinct from his own convictions:

There is little room for the luxury of gestures. President Giscard may talk about "an independent and strong Europe" but where is its military security, and where the protection for its oil and trade routes, if not still in Washington? Bonn understands this, which is why, even in its despair of Washington, it does not march to the seductive piping of President Giscard. Certainly President Giscard understands it too, but French politics forbid him to acknowledge it in public, even if he wanted to. Yet in Washington it is the unreality of these public postures that causes so much irritation.

Obviously, for *The Times*, the reassertion of Atlantic unity should take precedence over all other considerations. In this, the newspaper's views coincided with those of the Foreign Office. Because of this coincidence, we might hope that *The Times* would invite distinguished foreigners (columnists, politicians, and the like) to write in its "guest columns" more often so that its readers could be directly informed about others' contrasting—and not so "official"—views.

For a more detailed tracing of *The Times'* editorial positions, I shall deal in turn with the several major continuing subjects of this period.

The Iranian Crisis. The Times published in April 1980 alone nine editorial leaders and six articles on issues relating to Iran. On the whole, *The Times* expressed a European point of view throughout the crisis; at no time was there any reference to the so-called Anglo-American special relationship. At the same time, *The Times* showed an extraordinary degree of support for the United States, without much accommodation to the more divergent views expressed in the other countries of the European Community. The general tone of its comments was, perhaps, more mature. It avoided any sneering or ridiculing of Washington policy (in contrast to many Continental, particularly French, newspapers). It was the tone of an older, wiser, and more experienced partner addressing an impetuous young associate. Progressively, however, *The Times'* tone became more strident and its considerations of American policy more severe, especially after the abortive U.S. attempt to liberate the hostages in Iran. All along, as the crisis developed, the editorial line of *The Times* followed two main themes: (1) the West, but primarily the United States, should give priority to the Afghanistan situation, because the game is not yet lost in Iran; (2) Europe has to play its part and contribute to the solution of problems in this area of the world.

What about the real feelings of the American people? On 4/12/80, Fred Emery, a former correspondent of *The Times* in Washington, wrote from the American capital that he was struck by "the angry frustration among responsible Americans towards the hostage ordeal. Its intensity must not be underestimated." According to Mr. Emery, this frustration was "threatening to poison alliance relationships." But three days later, his views were contradicted by no less than *The Times'* editor.

William Rees-Mogg, in a special article (4/15/80), said that he did not believe that the American people were becoming so angry "that President Carter would be forced to take some action, even if unwise, to appease that anger." He thought that "the genuine and broad American public opinion was more self-confident, more rational and more restrained" than "some leader writers and gossips at Washington cocktail parties." Mr. Rees-Mogg was convinced that the American public "saw the main threat to America and to the future freedom of the world coming from Russian expansion":

The American people see that the detention of the hostages is an outrage . . . but very few of them want to take steps which would actually make the situation worse. The President is free to be patient, as he has been so far, and his allies are free to continue to counsel patience. They must, however, recognize that they will have to pay a very heavy price in loss of American confidence if they are seen to condone Russian aggression in Afghanistan.

One of the regular contributors to *The Times*, Geoffrey Smith, in an analysis of British political opinion (4/18/80), concluded that "there is almost certainly a majority in the House of Commons for action simply to reassure the Americans, even though there would probably be no majority for such action on its merits." And he went on: "It is not a bad test of any connexion when people are prepared to do something against their judgment for its sake."

On 4/30/80, *The Times* emphasized further the important role Europe should play in the circumstances. But how could Europe give steady support to a "troubled and angry American nation" if the European countries "squabbled among themselves?" That was why *The Times* was critical of Mrs. Thatcher for rejecting the compromise offered her in Luxembourg for Britain's contribution to the EEC's budget:

> Mrs. Thatcher, oddly in view of her feelings about world affairs, chose to take the narrow domestic view. She is guilty of misjudgment. The essential thing is to pull Europe and the alliance together; she has held Europe apart.

Simultaneously, *The Times* argued:

> Europe must also attempt to maintain communications with Moscow on behalf of the alliance. This is not appeasement but simple common sense.
> . . .
> Europe also has to frame a joint policy towards the Middle East, on which the future prosperity and peace of Europe depends.

In this context, *The Times* deplored the "little England attitudes struck in the House of Commons—which make Britain seem so ludicrously insular and chauvinist," and regretted Mrs. Thatcher's mistake "of rejecting large concessions and sending Chancellor Schmidt and President Giscard home angry and alienated." This, wrote *The Times*, showed "lack of judgment, a failure to put first things first."

Britain, the European Community, and the United States. Obviously, for *The Times*, Chancellor Schmidt was the European to trust. At the same time, *The Times* (6/13/80) opposed those Germans "who want Europe to reassert itself as a diplomatic power to fill the gap left by faltering America," and those, even "less responsible, [who] hope that Europe can be preserved as an island of detente while America alone carries the burden of patrolling its borders and protecting its vital lines to markets and raw materials."

In a special article from Bonn (7/22/80), Patricia Clough mentioned the deteriorating German-American relationship—the "deep tensions between the two most powerful countries of the West, the two key members of the alliance":

> Geography explains a lot. The Germans, many of whom have lived through one, if not two, devastating wars, know that they would probably be the ones to die in a third—and the fear of war here is very real. Similarly the Americans, way out of reach, attach less importance, it is felt, to negotiating a balanced reduction of medium range nuclear missiles than the Germans, at whom they are aimed.

But despite such differences, leading her to conclude, "The honeymoon is over," Clough denied that West Germans were turning anti-American:

> [Their] loyalty lies not only in the knowledge that their security depends on United States protection. The same instinct, or sense of affinity, which at the end of the war prompted millions of Germans to flee from the approaching Soviet army to the Americans in the West still prevails.

Commenting about the EEC Venice summit, *The Times* in a previous editorial (6/14/80) was satisfied that Britain's dispute with other community members had been settled "for the time being," and "Venice may turn out to be the beginning of a new phase":

> At any rate it could be said that a certain awareness of natural justice is beginning to seep into discussions where previously the Community rules were treated as sacrosanct. . . .
> There is time—though not much—to look more calmly at the inner workings of the Community, most of which are still geared to a Community of six. And there are now better conditions for examining together the position of the Community in the world. If the Community can now forgo the temptation to blame everything on the United States, it could grow into a sense of responsibility which could strengthen rather than weaken the alliance.

The North-South Diaglogue. The relations between the industrialized countries and the developing world have always drawn the attention of *The Times*. In response to "the Brandt Commission's suggestion of a summit meeting at which the industrialized countries and the oil producers could discuss concerted measures to rescue the third world," *The Times* (6/24/80) regretted that pending elections in three major industrial countries prevented the European Seven from acting on it:

> But no one should be allowed to forget the urgency of this problem, and preparatory work should go ahead on it with a view to holding a conference in the second half of next year. . . . It should not be held up by side-issues such as whether the Soviet block is invited, which should be approached pragmatically. The Soviet Union, as a major industrial power, undoubtedly shares responsibility for helping the Third World and should not be excluded if it appears willing to shoulder that responsibility. But so long as its idea of helping the Third World is to impose unpopular regimes by military force, it must be doubted whether it has anything worthwhile to contribute.

In its editorial of 7/10/80, however, *The Times* complained that the American administration, or more precisely Congress, was much more concerned with the military than with the moral balance of power. Quoting President Carter's 5/22/77 speech at Notre Dame University, where he called on the Soviet Union "to join in playing a larger role in aiding the developing world," *The Times* noted that nothing much came of this "noble vision." "Little more is heard of seeking Soviet cooperation. . . . And American development aid drifts downwards as a proportion of G.N.P." The editorial was very critical of the United States:

> The report of the Brandt commission on north-south relations, which argued cogently that aid was not to be seen as charity but as necessary for the survival of civilization, was almost wholly ignored by the American press and has sold only 6,000 copies in the United States, compared with 40,000 in Britain. . . .
> This is a dangerous trend in American affairs. It is understandable as a reaction to some of the bad investments of the past, and to the naive belief that American money could always buy allies, but the swing is going too far.

After noting that the United States devoted only 0.19 percent of its GNP to development assistance, compared with 0.52 percent for Britain, *The Times* concluded: "The United States is in some ways rightly disappointed by the failure of the Europeans to support it in its global responsibilities, but in that area it is barely even following where it ought to be leading."

On the other hand, *The Times* did not follow up on this line, and there were no comments when the British government in its formal assessment of the Brandt report belittled its importance while at the same time playing up the role of market forces.

The U.S. Elections: During August, 1980, the electoral campaign in the United States practically monopolized *The Times'* attention. Its coverage of the conventions was extensive, but editorially, *The Times* showed restraint in its assessment of the candidates. Still, it displayed more— sometimes positive, sometimes negative—interest in Mr. Reagan, the challenger, and his policies, particularly his foreign policy. After Mr. Reagan's nomination as the Republican candidate, *The Times* devoted an editorial to his personality and his thinking in domestic and foreign affairs. "Mr. Reagan's words have sometimes been less reassuring than his record," *The Times* said (7/17/80):

> There have been times when the loose expression of his sentiments have appeared to confirm the impression of a right-wing extremist. There have been rather more occasions when they have seemed to cast doubt on whether he has a grip on some of the principal problems facing the country.

But then *The Times* went to some lengths to put the best possible construction on Mr. Reagan's stance on military strength and arms control:

> His assertion that the United States ought to have military superiority over the Soviet Union would be a cause of anxiety if it had to be taken at face value. . . .
> To demand military superiority as an objective designed both to persuade the American people to make the necessary investments to secure parity, and to convince the Soviet Union that it needs to negotiate seriously, is not a mark of political bravado. Indeed, it is an example of the course that has served the West well during the postwar years of seeking to negotiate from strength.

In that editorial, Mr. Reagan appeared to emerge as the more desirable candidate: "It would be reasonable to expect the collective operation of the Presidency under his control to be more effective than it has been during the Carter years."

According to Louis Heren (7/5/80), former correspondent in Washington and now Deputy Editor of *The Times,* Mr. Reagan's advisers were convinced that he "would make a prudent and pragmatic president who would model himself on President Eisenhower." They thought he would restore American military strength and favor "a permanent American presence in the Middle East":

> [S]ome of his advisers are thinking of bases for American air squadrons in Sinai, Egypt and Oman. This would be an extraordinary extension of American power which, after the Vietnam misadventure, seems hardly likely to win an election.
> One is left wondering if he knows what his advisers are planning for him.

Mr. Heren had doubts about the extent of Mr. Reagan's interest in foreign affairs: "His habit of two or three naps a day does not suggest a vigorous man determined to reassert American leadership."

In a general assessment of the election campaign up through 9/30/80, *The Times* criticized Governor Reagan for "re-arousing all the old fears that the American voters had":

> His style has elements of innocence and eccentricity. He puts together half-remembered facts and half-understood propositions with the utmost charm and good humour. . . .
>
> So far . . . he has portrayed himself in the very terms in which the Democrats want to portray him.

As for his incumbent opponent, said *The Times:*

> President Carter sounds much more sensible. But the reality is not much more reassuring.
>
> . . . [He] talks perfectly good sense, but his reasonable words and good intentions are somehow converted into unsuccessful politics.

So where does *The Times* come out this time?

> Governor Reagan does not sound sensible at all. He strikes the particular note of those old gentlemen who used to say that their grandchildren could paint better than Picasso, the note of the old fuddy duddy. In such a contest, the advantage seems to be swinging in favour of the candidate who at least appears to talk sense.

The Times' tilt toward President Carter emerged again in an editorial on "Going for the Jewish Vote" (9/6/80). Mr. Reagan was judged "crude" on the issue, while Mr. Carter was seen to be making subtle but critical distinctions:

> Mr. Reagan made a hard, somewhat crude pitch for Jewish sympathies, deploring the Carter Administration's failure to back up current Israeli policies. . . . "Israel is a major strategic asset to America", Mr. Reagan told B'nai B'rith, "and to weaken Israel is to destabilize the Middle East."
>
> This may have been what his audience wanted to hear, but it ignores the fact that what has largely obstructed the peace process, with the attendant risk of "destabilization", is the attitude adopted by Mr. Begin and his colleagues. . . .
>
> In fact, what President Carter has tried to do is to distinguish between support for the existence of Israel as such, and support for some of the less helpful policies of the present Israeli Government.
>
> Whether Jewish American voters will make that distinction in November is another matter. . . . The concern of those elsewhere in the world is that it

should not cause things to be said or commitments entered into by the candidates which might damage the effectiveness of the United States as a broker for peace in the Middle East.

Such was the sleuthing a reader had to do to try to determine where *The Times* stood in the choice for U.S. president. In this matter as in others, one too often found in *The Times'* editorials—between all the considerations on the one hand and then on the other—reason to despair of getting any unambiguous recommendations of what should be done and who would be best to do it. Nonetheless, as I said in beginning this general appreciation, I could not understand the British view of the world without it.

Response to Pierre

Target Readership

Henri Pierre called *The Times* "an important working tool for Britain's elite—for journalists, academics, leaders generally," but then asked whether that should be the newspaper's function. In his view, "*The Times* should direct itself to the needs of the *average* reader."

And so it does, maintained Charles Douglas-Home, *The Times'* Foreign Editor. If *The Times* aims at a particular sort of reader, he said, it is "the sixth-former"—that is, someone around age 18 just about to leave school. But he admitted, not without pride, that surveys reveal *The Times'* readers to be greatly concentrated among the professions, making up "a mosaic of minority interests." In terms of mission, *The Times*, he said, tries first to report the day's news, then to provide "a service for the student of contemporary history a year from now."

The Times' coverage of the U.S. election year provoked differing judgments of just whom *The Times* served and how well. Henri Pierre observed that, for *The Times* (as for many American newspapers and voters), the choice between Carter and Reagan was a perplexing prospect. In Pierre's opinion, *The Times'* response was to offer too much—rather, "too rich"—coverage. The points of the stories, he said, tended to get lost in small details. He felt that the editorials were sometimes helpful (such as Peter Jay's on the limitations of the power of the presidency), sometimes not (such as one so in praise of Carter "as to be a reward for a good dinner"). The worst aspect, he said, was the hardship imposed on the reader trying to figure out where *The Times* stood in the matter. The typical piece, according to his paraphase, went like this: "Carter was right on this, that, and so on. . . . But he has failed to command confidence. . . . Reagan has the capacity to persuade, and other favorable traits. . . . But with so much uncertainty in current affairs, we might be better off with continuity in Washington."

"Honestly," said Pierre, "I was lost."

On hearing this, Mort Rosenblum of the *International Herald Tribune* asked, "Did you read *The New York Times'* endorsement of Carter? It went on the same way for 42 inches."

Douglas-Home denied that *The Times'* coverage was too rich: "We don't expect people to read it all." Speaking personally, he said that the occasion is rare when a newspaper should declare its interest in seeing one candidate win over others; but when it does, it should do so early, not hold back its choice "theatrically" until just before the election.

As *The Times* approached the Carter-Reagan contest, William Rees-Mogg, the editor, toured the United States and wrote a piece that had the effect, Douglas-Home said, of "making Reagan respectable." But subsequently, even when *The Times* editorially criticized Carter's performance in office, it balked at accepting the consequence of this judgment—that is, endorsing Reagan. Henri Pierre's confusion over where *The Times* stood reflected *The Times'* own confusion.

Expanding on his sense of *The Times'* role in British society, Douglas-Home, speaking of the labor-management dispute that had shut down the newspaper for months, said, "When *The Times* wasn't publishing, the whole of the British press was diminished; the collective output suffered. When we are publishing, we contribute to the nation's debate. We help to define the very area of discussion."

If what contemporary media criticism has called "the agenda-setting function of the press" needs evidence that this is what editors themselves think they are doing, one could hardly ask for a more explicit acknowledgment than Douglas-Home's, "We help to define the very area of discussion."

Reporting and Opinion

From its foreign correspondents, *The Times* expects, above all, new information, not opinion. He may be severe, Douglas-Home admitted, in believing that correspondents should not personalize their reports—beyond exercising the choice of subject. He agreed it would be pointless to pay them simply to duplicate what the news agencies (Reuters, United Press International, Associated Press) already provide. On the other hand, he argued that the agency material is either just not good enough to rely on or is in a style that is not right for *The Times*. In regard to letting correspondents venture further into comment, he said he was trying to get labeled commentaries placed on the news pages.

"When there are lapses in our foreign reporting," Douglas-Home explained, "often they occur simply because the right man is away when something newsworthy happens. But, in my perhaps heretical view, it doesn't matter if you don't get it right on a particular day. The flow over time is the important thing."

How much the foreign correspondent himself (or, more rarely, herself) sets the agenda for the discussion of U.S.–European relations or other issues was a question that reflected partly on the journalist, partly on his or her working conditions. William Pfaff, a writer for the *International Herald Tribune* and *The New Yorker*, was troubled by the apparent lack of detachment in the work of *The Times'* correspondents in the United States: "They seem to think they are parts of the process, advocates even, as if they have become the insiders—or gone native."

Douglas-Home allowed, "Yes, there's a corrupting ambience in Washington. A journalist there is socially respectable, and you can't escape in those circles the fact that you're either a leaker or a person leaked to. It gets very close."

Mort Rosenblum thought that this was a problem everywhere, but Peregrine Worsthorne of the London *Sunday Telegraph* believed that *The Times* would face a very particular problem in covering the U.S. political situation now that Reagan was president and the Senate was under Republican control. For a whole generation, he argued, the foreign correspondents for *The Times* and other European newspapers have been liberal in their personal politics, and their contacts in the United States have been with liberals too. (He recalled an occasion in Washington years ago when Joe Alsop could joke to his guests, "I hope you won't be offended, but I've a Republican coming to dinner.")

"Every *Times* reporter and the whole *Times* establishment," Worsthorne contended, "are Democratic Party sympathizers. How will they manage now? One of their main tasks will be to improve their lines to the great patriotic majority in America that has decided to find its voice again." Moreover, in his view, what to *The Times* will be a journalistic problem will be to Europe a bigger challenge: "One can imagine that this Republican majority, which the European press has regarded as philistine, as beneath European notice, or has totally ignored ever since the Roosevelt coalition came to power, will now find the allies rather more of a nuisance than an advantage. They may even get on more easily with the Soviet Union, which is another great nationalistic body."

The problem of access to a different group of politicians, replied Douglas-Home, "is simply something cyclical. Once they get into government, they become porous." A greater source of difficulty, he felt, was the correspondents' lack of preparation for dealing with subjects requiring a specialist's knowledge. Since Britain abolished conscription, for example, no one with first-hand military experience—that is, no ex-conscript—has come into journalism; the coverage of military matters is the poorer for that.

To break out of what he granted was the Washington "hothouse—it's not a grassroots source," Douglas-Home would, "in an ideal case, post a *Times* 'social' reporter on the West Coast, not in New York City. But a correspondent feels disembodied out there because of the time-zone disparity with the newspaper's publishing schedule." Even had *The Times* posted correspondents at a distance from Washington, the election result might have been no less surprising. "You can't expect journalists," said Douglas-Home, "to predict election outcomes any better than political practitioners."

Labeling the Difference

The concern for maintaining the distinction between straight reporting and the correspondent's opinion was confined to the British and American journalists. Eugene Blabey, Vice-President and General Manager for United Press International's operations in Europe, attributed this to different cultural expectations—the British versus the French, or even more broadly, the Anglo-American versus the Continental, approaches to writing for and to reading a newspaper. The U.S. and British tradition attempts to put the writer at a distance from what is being written about, while the way of the Continental writer is to tell you what he or she thinks, and the more individualistic he or she is in doing that, the better. A reader accustomed to the Anglo-American approach will judge Continental stories to be short on facts; the Continental reader will find the Anglo-American version dry and boring.

The Anglo-American reaction to the limitations of the "objective" reporting tradition is to permit opinion but to give it a label—to make explicit for the reader what is "news" and what is "comment." It was along this line that William Pfaff urged Douglas-Home "to allow *The Times'* foreign correspondents the occasional thousand words to explain what's going on."

While not rejecting the idea altogether, Douglas-Home warned that "the idea of the 'definitive piece' is anathema—we shouldn't do a subject once: we should go back to it time and again."

Mort Rosenblum said that the *International Herald Tribune* deals with the distinction by presenting no fewer than four different categories of editorial material: straight reporting; news analysis; an "Insights" page; and the editorial page—all labeled, if not implicitly clear, for what they are.

Eugene Blabey found it useful to distinguish even among editorials, marking off those that simply try to explain from those that try to convince. In this connection, he defended *The Times* editorials that had so bewildered Henri Pierre. They were, in Blabey's view, properly "educational." He asked, "Why *should* a newspaper take a stand on an election abroad in which its readers cannot even vote?"

Melvin Lasky of *Encounter* pointed to another way of categorizing editorial matter. "If *The Times* itself does not seem so full-bodied as the *Frankfurter Allgemeine Zeitung*," he said, "that's because they ghettoize their good special coverage in *The Times Supplements*." The supplements, of which *The Times Literary Supplement* is most famous, are published separately from *The Times* and from *The Sunday Times*.

Prospects

At the time these comments were offered, *The Times, The Sunday Times*, the *Supplements*, and a book publishing division faced the possibility of being sold and split up—and *The Times* itself, the most financially troubled part of the enterprise, shut down for good—given the then owners' declaration they could no longer go on.

Douglas-Home reflected on the steps taken and not taken that preceded and perhaps contributed to the crisis. For three years, until the attempt was abandoned in 1970, *The Times* tried to become a seven-day-a-week operation, in effect, "a daily *Sunday Times*" (a paper much bigger and more varied than its daily namesake). During those years it was decided to co-locate the physical plant of *The Times* and *The Sunday Times*, even though *The Times* went on to accept being a "low-circulation newspaper of record." Labor costs hit *The Times* particularly hard, most dramatically illustrated by the strike that shut down the paper for months starting in November 1978.

It was for him a source of regret, said Douglas-Home, that what proved then to be a temporary shutdown was not taken as an opportunity to "review *The Times*' rituals," but "the prevailing sense of insecurity was expressed in a disinclination to change." Perhaps it was insecurity again that made the idea of trying to be "less boring" seem "equal to the lowering of standards."

Whether or not *The Times* needs, as Henri Pierre insisted, more stories "that are alive!" is perhaps a matter of taste.

Jerome Dumoulin of *L'Express*, however, agreed with his compatriot: " 'Boring' is, alas, the word for *The Times*."

"It's boring to you," retorted Peregrine Worsthorne, "because it's not addressed to you. It's the house organ of Britain's political class. For us the letters from readers are the opposite of 'boring'. What we find interesting is not likely to appeal to readers abroad. The obituaries, for example, are little bits of literature. *The Times* is a gem to the social historian. It's the spirit of Jane Austen found every day in the newspaper."

"But what *are* supposed to be interesting, namely, the opinion pieces," replied William Pfaff, "are precisely what's boring."

To the contrary, said Mort Rosenblum with a touch of mischief, "I find *The Times* sensational. It's *Le Monde* that puts me to sleep."

Rupert Murdoch, owner of *The New York Post* and other newspapers around the world, came to *The Times'* financial rescue under a purchase agreement pledging that *The Times* would and should continue in its historically established way. Trusting that assurance from an entrepreneur whose tabloid properties, with their sensation-mongering headlines, would offer daily offense to a *Times* reader, was better than having no *Times* at all. Thus *The Times* survives for the moment, still in substance if not in ownership a uniquely British expression of the cultivated life.

—MR

chapter four

LE MONDE: De Gaulle's Only Legitimate Heir

Pierre Salinger*

Brief History

L*e Monde* was founded in December 1944 on the specific request of General Charles de Gaulle that in the immediate postwar period there be a serious journal of record in France. It was to replace *Le Temps,* which had been forbidden by the French resistance to reappear.

The government handed to the founders of *Le Monde* the building and printing plant of *Le Temps* on the Rue des Italiens (where *Le Monde* still operates) and also gave it the money to get started. Two men who were extremely important in putting *Le Monde* on the street—Pierre-Henri Teitgen, de Gaulle's Minister of Information, and Gaston Palewski, the general's chef de cabinet—had the idea that the newspaper would unofficially reflect French foreign policy. For many years, readers of *Le Monde* could read certain articles on foreign policy with the assurance that they had been instigated by the government. That is much less true today although the official thinking of the Quai D'Orsay is not absent from the columns of *Le Monde.* The original director of the newspaper was Hubert Beuve-Mery, who ceded his role to Jacques Fauvet in December of 1969 after 25 years at the helm of the newspaper.

The role of General de Gaulle in the founding of the newspaper has

---

*Paris Correspondent, ABC News

not been without effect over the years in the treatment of the news. It is not only that the general remains a point of reference even now for *Le Monde,* with the question often being posed, "What would the general have done if he were here today?" The powerful position of *Le Monde* has also created around it a stubborn and often vehement opposition. *Le Monde* itself is extremely sensitive to criticism and not noted for admitting major error.

I was struck at a press conference soon after moving to Paris when, at the end of a long period of questioning, a rather arrogant young man got up and said: "As usual, it is up to the representative of *Le Monde* to ask a serious question." Jean-Marie Domenach, writing in *L'Esprit,* once said: "The bad thing is the monopoly. When a newspaper has become the compendium of French culture, the monitor of intelligence and French politics, when nothing really counts unless it has appeared in *Le Monde,* that is an unhealthy situation in a regime of liberty, and unhealthy for *Le Monde* itself." Finally, the historic orientation of the newspaper from its founding to today has been nationalistic and, in a way, neutralist.

All through its history, its two favorite targets have been the United States and West Germany. From decrying the dangers of "Coca-Cola imperialism" in the 1950s (in an article written by Beuve-Mery himself), the columns of *Le Monde* have expanded to decry all forms of American "imperialism," particularly during the time that Claude Julien was the head of the foreign affairs section of *Le Monde.* Claude Julien took his basic anti-American sentiments to *Le Monde Diplomatique* and has now been named as the successor of Jacques Fauvet when the latter retires in 1982.

Le Monde is undoubtedly the most important and prestigious daily newspaper in France. It is also a newspaper that leaves very few of its readers indifferent. The emotions raised by *Le Monde* range from uncritical adoration to sheer hate, for the newspaper has a clear point of view that it expresses with insistence, and in a manner that some consider heavy-handed. For an American reader, *Le Monde* (and for that matter the rest of the French press) differs from what one is accustomed to reading in the written media in the United States. American newspapers make an effort, mostly successful, to separate opinion and information. Opinion is labeled as such, often confined to special pages of the newspaper reserved for that purpose. The rest of the newspaper is devoted to information. No one can pretend that this information is without bias. Every journalist brings to his work the sum of his own experience and prejudices. But given that undeniable fact, American newspapers stress pure information.

Every young journalist who learns his trade in the United States is insistently reminded that the reader is not interested in his personal point of view on the story he is writing. "Just give them the facts," my city editor used to growl repeatedly when I was making my first paths in journalism in the mid-1940s. The tradition in France is just the opposite. Journalists are encouraged to mix information and opinion, and those who do not have a point of view are often considered dull or unreadable. This is particularly true of *Le Monde,* where opinion and information are mixed with great skill and determination. More than that, the *Le Monde* correspondent very often draws a conclusion to his story, rather than letting the reader do it for himself. Finally, reporters for *Le Monde* have a tendency to moralize, which is exasperating for a foreign reader.

But all this is a part of the centuries-old tradition of the French press and cannot in itself constitute a fatal criticism of *Le Monde.* When the young George Clemenceau went to America in the mid-1860s as a stringer for *Le Temps,* the predecessor of *Le Monde,* he wrote a series of remarkable articles on the impeachment of President Andrew Johnson that contained all the ingredients of opinion, conclusion, and moralization that I have described, yet remained an important document on how a foreigner saw one of the most dramatic manifestations of the Constitution of the United States.

Le Monde, however, is not just a vehicle for the dissemination of information about today's events around the world. It is also a receptacle for debate—"le discours," as it is called in French. Subjects of society, economy, actuality are debated in the pages of *Le Monde* by people totally outside the craft of journalism—educators, politicians, philosophers, workers, representing a wide spectrum of opinion in France. But it should also be noted that on basic political subjects—for example, during our period of study, the policies of French President Valery Giscard d'Estaing and Prime Minister Raymond Barre—*Le Monde* frequently calls on commentators outside its own staff who will either make arguments the newspaper itself is not prepared to make or will further *Le Monde's* general line of opposition to the policies of the government while at the same time adding credibility to *Le Monde's* own positions. An example of this policy was the frequent use of articles by Michel Debre, a close associate of General de Gaulle and a former French prime minister who vociferously opposed the policies of the Giscard d'Estaing government.

One final observation before coming to our subject. Some people complain that *Le Monde* is a leftist newspaper. It is true that its staff includes confirmed Marxists, but it would be simplistic to attach the "leftist" label to the newspaper. *Le Monde* is a nationalistic newspaper, stridently so, and its leftist tendencies (and they do exist) seem to manifest themselves in almost exact proportions to the number of kilometers from Paris of the country whose problems are being treated by a *Le Monde* journalist. Possibly the most unbalanced coverage one finds in *Le Monde* is its view of Latin America, habitually tinged by the revolutionary and leftist slant of its reporters who treat the matters of that continent.

Le Monde's *View of U.S.–European and U.S.–French Relations*

The above background is necessary to get to the heart of the subject assigned to us: how *Le Monde* covers and perceives the relationship between the United States and Europe. To this I myself have added the subject of how *Le Monde* sees relations between France and the United States because it is inextricably interwoven with the central subject. *Le Monde*, despite its evolution since its foundation in the days after World War II, continues to have a Gaullien view of the universe, in which France is at the very center. Logically, therefore, *Le Monde* takes a special view of France's role in Europe that makes its own view of French relations with the United States as important as its view of European relations with the United States. This is heightened by the fact that General de Gaulle withdrew France from the military apparatus of the Atlantic Alliance—the North Atlantic Treaty Organization.

Thus, on a political and military level, *Le Monde* frequently reacts to transatlantic relationships or crisis by giving us its version of the French response and the NATO response as two distinct and separate things. Complicating this analysis is the growing vision of *Le Monde* (and the French government as well) that the future stability of Europe relies on a special relationship between France and the Federal Republic of Germany, and *Le Monde*'s (and the French government's) continuing view that Great Britain will always be an American Trojan horse inside Europe, a nation not to be trusted to have basic European tendencies.

The period under study was rich with events that were subject to analysis by *Le Monde* on the European–U.S. relationship and the French–U.S. relationship. They included the crisis between the United States and Iran, the continuing effort to bring about the release of the American hostages, and the American demand that its European allies impose sanctions on Iran. There were the Soviet intervention in Afghanistan and the U.S.–European contre-temps on how to react to that invasion. This, of course, included President Carter's efforts to bring about the boycott of the Moscow Olympic games and the European and French reaction to that effort. There were the NATO decision to modernize its nuclear forces, the European initiative on the Middle East, the argument over whether Europe is in the process of Finlandization. There was a very special debate in France on what is perceived as an Anglo-Saxon assault on the French language and French culture. And, of course, there was all through the period of our study *Le Monde*'s perception of the American election process and the candidates seeking the presidency. I shall treat these subjects one by one before trying to draw a final conclusion on *Le Monde*'s perception of the U.S.–European and U.S.–French relationships.

U.S.–Europe, U.S.–France, Finlandization

Two important themes occurred again and again in *Le Monde* with reference to the relations between the United States and Europe and the United States and France. To paraphrase the first: in view of the present weakness of the United States, it is time for the Europeans to pursue their independent policies. And the second, an eternal refrain of *Le Monde:* what would General de Gaulle have done under today's conditions?

Let us look at two editorials of *Le Monde* on this subject. The first (4/17/80) says that even if it might be "exaggerated" to refer to current transatlantic relations as a crisis, it would be a mistake to attribute to the current situation the idea that it is a "new phenomenon":

> The diverse and recent international crises have only reawakened a sickness latent since its origins, progressively aggravated these last years by changes that have appeared on the world scene. The Atlantic alliance was founded more than 30 years ago on the basis of a fact—the crushing superiority of the United States in a world that had just divided itself into two blocs—and with a fundamental objective, to prevent a frontal attack by the Soviet Union on Western Europe. The relations at the interior of this Alliance remained fundamentally unequal, but Europe, in exchange for the protection offered, had no choice but to accept the *fait accompli*—generally military—imposed by the United States.

The editorial continues:

> The weakness of the American positions has profoundly modified this situation: on the economic front, the reestablishment of Europe contrasting with the weakness of the dollar and the decline of productivity in the United States, has led to an increase of the political weight of the Old Continent and the diversification of its interests in a world that has become multipolar. On the military level, the strengthening of Soviet power dissuades more and more the United States from reacting with as much force as it did in the past, even when its interests are directly menaced. Washington has up to now replaced gunboat diplomacy with economic and

diplomatic sanctions, but that approach can only be effective if it receives the support of the other countries. The paradox of all this is that the United States today has more and more reason to need its allies, just at the moment when these (the allies) have every reason to consider her policies less credible.

Le Monde concludes:

The Afghan crisis has demonstrated a counterpart phenomenon: the Europeans had become used to basing their security on a defense of dissuasion—essentially American, and on political détente—largely national. They worry about the second element being in danger as the Americans ask their support to "punish" Moscow by nonmilitary means. The loud protestations of pro-American solidarity that one hears in the most faithful capitals like London and Bonn contrast with the political and legal quibbles advanced in Paris. But they cannot replace either the decisive actions demanded by Washington nor eclipse the fundamental problem: the Atlantic edifice, founded to cure the postwar tensions, is only able to react rather poorly to the tensions of the '80s.

On 5/15/80, in an editorial on the American pressures related to Iran, Afghanistan, and the Olympic games, *Le Monde* goes further:

The Europeans believe therefore that it would be wise for the moment to wait allowing the situation to develop while maintaining a certain pressure on Teheran. In Naples, they will confirm their decision not to sign any more contracts with Teheran and should—and this will be the most delicate— decide their positions in contracts already in effect. The excuse for this avoidance of responsibility resides, of course, in Washington's incoherence. But, shouldn't the Nine seize this occasion to affirm a policy of their own and declare . . . what appears to them ill-fated and what they judge necessary?

André Fontaine, in an article on the problem of the transatlantic relationship (4/16/80), poses the question of what General de Gaulle would have done under the circumstances. Noting that the French government appears to be giving its support to the United States on a "drop-by-drop" basis, and that France was the only country to send its ambassador to the May Day ceremonies in Moscow despite the events in Afghanistan, Fontaine writes:

There is no absence, among the heirs of the men of June 18, of those good spirits to point out that [this policy] is but a caricature of Gaullism, explained by the fear of losing the holy petroleum, by the fear of defying Moscow at the apogee of its military strength, and by electoral considerations. Those argue that the General, like Mao, believed that when the two imperialisms faced off, the wise thing to do was to support the weaker to better resist the stronger. America having for several years swallowed a series of grass snakes, it is she that we should encourage to hold on as during the Berlin and Cuba crises. It is always dangerous to make the dead speak, especially when they have not left a political testament. Nobody can say with certainty what General de Gaulle would have done under the current circumstances . . . but it is difficult to doubt that he would have had the same feelings as his actual successor for the disconcerting personality, to say the least, of President Carter. All the more so, given that the damned soul of Carter, Zbigniew Brzezinski, was a relentless anti-Gaullist (his writings at the time he was a professor at Columbia are testimony).

Fontaine concludes on the same theme as the *Le Monde* editorial cited above:

For the thirty years it has lasted, the dialogue among the superpowers has proved that it is impotent to resolve the essential problems of our time. . . . It is high time that the voice of Europe, which for a long time has understood the hard way how the enterprises of domination work, makes itself heard. If the Europeans engage themselves on that road, they are assured of the active support of their peoples, who do not resign themselves easily to passivity and decadence, and of the immense majority of the Third World, which has abandoned all the illusions it could have had on the wisdom or the disinterest of the superpowers.

In the issue of 6/4/80, Thierry de Montbrial, Director of the French Institute of Foreign Relations, echoes the same theme. Saying that it is not surprising that the "transatlantic misunderstanding" has taken "proportions without precedent," Montbrial says the Europeans "accuse President Carter of all the capital sins, with proof in hand." Montbrial pursues: "The Europeans must not consider that the reestablishment of a 'structure of peace' rests completely on the Americans. It must understand that the decline of relative weight of the United States, without doubt irreversible, creates the necessity of the affirmation of a European pillar, coherent, independent, but allied to the United States."

A slightly different tune comes in the 4/25/80 article of Jacques Mallet, the national secretary of the CDS (Centre des Démocrates Sociaux), one of the small centrist parties in the government coalition:

Here, the United States calls, in a most pressing way, for solidarity. True. But can we remain deaf to their call? It would be to forget the essential; the Atlantic Alliance remains indispensable for our security. . . . Solidarity does not signify submission or alignment. It does not require the adoption by all our countries of all the measures taken or projected by the United States. But it does require decisions showing in an unequivocal way the willingness of the Europeans to help their American allies in this difficult phase.

And Jean Laloy, a former French Ambassador, writes in *Le Monde* of 4/18/80:

Let us come back to reality. Every serious international crisis implicates Western Europe and the United States together. If the relations at the interior of the alliance are bad, as they were at the time of Suez in 1956, the dangers ride . . . if the relations are good, the risks recede. Remember the Cuban crisis and that of Berlin. Today the relations in the alliance are bad, and risks in the days ahead are becoming worse.

Professor Alfred Grosser, one of the keenest students of the relations among the members of the Atlantic Alliance, and a frequent contributor to *Le Monde*, writes in the edition of 5/13–14/80:

What the American press writes is not exact. It is not true that the tension between the United States and its European allies is the worst since 1945. The real new factor is the United States and the consequences that flow from that. Not simply or principally the weakness of their president, nor the desperate sadness of the choice offered to the most lucid of American voters. Much more serious is the real weakness of its capacity to exert leverage on its permanent and principal adversary, which can take over a new country with total impunity, and also on a smaller and occasional adversary that can safely risk taking fifty hostages and keeping them for six months.

Grosser himself yields to *Le Monde*'s constant reference to General de Gaulle: "Each time the United States found itself in a position of inferiority with respect to the Soviet Union, General de Gaulle played the card of solidarity before his desire to affirm [French independence] in the face of an ally. Today, to talk about [France's] independence means to keep its distance from its ally."

Still, having often issued the clarion call for Europe to seize the opportunity and devise its own path in the face of the evident weakness of the United States, a certain prudence injects itself into *Le Monde*'s editorial of 7/13–14/80:

With regard to the superpowers, "the role of Europe in the world" that Mr. Giscard d'Estaing and Mr. Schmidt call for is not for the purpose of replacing the United States nor to differentiate itself systematically, but to choose in all circumstances in the context of European interests and with an appraisal of the strengths and weaknesses of the American ally the policy which it judges best. The role of Europe cannot be the search for appeasement at any price, and the USSR would be living in illusion—if it is not already—in thinking that the policy of Europe can be neutrality. Europe is too exposed to remain outside a world conflict. Playing its role, having its own policies, implies that Europe must accept its responsibilities in all fields, and that requires giving itself the means. That is the opposite of resignation.

Maurice Delarue, another *Le Monde* stalwart, looks at the growing concern in the United States over the "failure" of its European allies to rally to certain American theses in an article on 6/19/80. Acknowledging that there is a rising sentiment in the United States that France is an "incorrigible and unsavable" ally, Delarue goes on: "If such judgments on France are not new—even if they are rarely described with such vivacity—the Americans are discovering today that the French 'perversity' is gaining ground in all of Europe. . . . Great Britain, it is true, always benefits from a certain indulgence. Mrs. Thatcher is a television star. Her frankness is a big hit and the bad tricks she plays on her partners in the European Community are usually put to her credit."

Reinforcing *Le Monde*'s view that England is treated as a "special case" in the United States, Delarue notes that it was "barely perceived" in the United States that the British had "decided before the French to go to the Olympic games in Moscow or that the government in London is sabotaging without discretion a major part of the European sanctions against Iran."

Having at length examined the Afghanistan crisis and noted in passing that the Afghan resistance "should look for help more from the Islamic world than from Western Europe"—which, he points out, would have the advantage of not transforming the Afghanistan crisis into an East-West confrontation—Delarue concludes: "Finally, many Europeans are persuaded that the Afghanistan crisis furnishes the opportunity for seeking a rapprochement between Western Europe and the Islamic world" for which, he says, the Americans are badly positioned. The Americans "should at least admit that in certain circumstances, it would be preferable if the United States and Europe were not aligned and played complementary roles."

Michel Debre, the former French prime minister and indefatigable contributor to *Le Monde,* takes all the above and puts it into a context that is purely French. And he comes back to his vision of France as the "lone horseman." "France was the lone horseman in rejecting the project of a European army. She was right. France was the lone horseman on deciding to build a nuclear strike force. She was right. France played the role of the lone horseman in deciding to leave the military apparatus of NATO and in inaugurating detente with the Soviet Union and recognizing China. Each time she was right. One of the motives that justifies the immense respect for the memory of General de Gaulle is that he retaught the Republic that it had to be a lone horseman when the circumstances required." But Debre pursues: "One must not, however, hide grave weaknesses behind a natural attitude. To be a lone horseman, one must have a clear objective ahead and a good mount."

Any discussion of the relationship between the United States and Europe would be incomplete without studying *Le Monde's* approach to the debate on the upgrading of NATO missiles, which in Europe is called the Euro-missile controversy. *Le Monde's* position is made clear in an editorial published on 4/27-28/80, which returns to the deeply felt regret that the defense of Europe is primarily in the hands of the Americans, and once again it goes back to the attitude of General de Gaulle.

Written in the aftermath of the failure of the American mission to rescue the hostages in Iran, the editorial says notably:

> The political disaster that the United States has just suffered in Iran can have a beneficial effect if the Europeans, at the very moment when the Community launches head first into one of the most serious crises in its history, draws the lessons it imposes; no one has the right, neither Europe, neither the states which make it up, nor the peoples, nor the individuals, to abdicate into anyone's hands—even the best motivated—to renounce the means of action it possesses and the capacity to use it freely. De Gaulle was convinced, and Mao, and many others before them. It is not a subject of isolation, of refusing aide and alliance, but of never forgetting that one can only assure one's security—that is to say one's future—by counting first on one's self and not in counting on the presumed wisdom of a pretended "leadership." It is, in fact, the best means not only of making oneself respected but of assuring one's friends and allies. . . . It is true that the Europeans are not in a position to assure by themselves their military security, even if in that domain the obstacles are much less technical than political. It is the absence of political will that has prevented Europe from creating a real armaments industry.

Le Monde concludes: "If Mr. Carter's error provokes among the Europeans a reaction that renders them conscious of their fragility, and convinces them that their fate is first in their hands, the unfortunate event will have served a good purpose."

On 6/14/80, Michel Tatu studies the defense proposals of the UDF (Union pour la Démocratie Française) and the RPR (Rassemblement pour la République), the two major parties of the government coalition:

> The only new objection one can make [to the RPR theories] concerns the future establishment of new medium-range American missiles on European soil. The Euro-strategic arms will reinforce the American umbrella by menacing Soviet soil with reprisals, while weakening indirectly the French deterrent force, in the measure that it copies it. If the Soviets go around this new NATO deterrent, it will cost them less to go around the French deter-

rent, which promises them comparable damage. It is quite evident that complete "Finlandization," that is to say, complete sovietization of the Federal Republic of Germany, would have dramatic consequences for France. The only question is what Paris can most usefully do to prevent this eventuality. A first option is to affirm a political solidarity without reserve, on announcing her guaranteed participation in any "battle of Germany" at the side of the Americans and other allies. The principal objection one can make to this thesis is that practically it does not modify the military conditions of the confrontation, thus rendering it neither more nor less possible than in the past while calling for a much greater defense effort both on the classic and nuclear level of tactics. The other option involves reinforcing the French nuclear deterrent in such a manner that the umbrella, thus created, extends little by little from France to her neighbors. That effort can be pursued alone, but it must not close the door to cooperation. One missed opportunity presented itself with the debate on the American Euro-missiles; the deployment of equivalent missiles constructed in cooperation by Paris and Bonn, the employment of which would be submitted to a Franco-German "double key," would have confirmed the widening of the French deterrent without the need to ask Germany to renounce its integration in NATO.

A *Le Monde* editorial of 7/19/80 concedes, however, that the deployment of 572 Pershing 2 and cruise missiles "will not suffice to reestablish the numerical superiority of the West."

Claude Bourdet, a leftist journalist and a leader of the left-fringe party, the Parti Socialist Unifie (PSU), and a frequent contributor to *Le Monde*, takes a contrary track in *Le Monde* of 4/25/80: "The European statesmen, at least in France and Germany, seem conscious of the current escalation (of nuclear weapons) but don't seem to have sufficient independence or political courage to oppose the depth of the American initiatives. Already, last autumn, the real balance of nuclear weapons in Europe has been arbitrarily cut up and falsified to bring about the acceptance of what is called the 'modernization' of NATO missiles."

On 5/14/80 on an opinion page, *Le Monde* printed a long analysis on the Euro-missile controversy by Soviet General Anatoli Gribikov in which he cites the classic Soviet arguments:

> The dangerous plans of NATO to relaunch the armaments race on the European continent, and in the first instance to install new American middle-range missiles on the soil of Western Europe, has the objective to destroy the equilibrium of forces that exists on the European continent, to obtain military superiority over the Warsaw Pact, and to prejudice the interests of the socialist countries and in general all the countries of Europe. This goes against the objectives of detente. The members of the Warsaw Pact cannot admit to such a thing.

Finally, a line on the "Finlandization debate." In an article on 6/20/80, André Fontaine poses the question of whether Mr. Giscard d'Estaing or Mr. Schmidt is the "most Finlandized" and rejects the charge against both. But he points out: "That spirit [Finlandization] does exist in those who govern France and the Federal Republic. The steps it has taken because of the American decline, notably on the military level, and the inconsistency of Mr. Carter, have really pushed them to seek accommodation with Moscow. There are many in the United States who would be ready to cry treason!"

U.S.–Iran

Our study of *Le Monde* started in April 1980, five months after the taking of the American hostages in Iran. Thus, it does not include the early reactions of *Le Monde* to that event. Still, that attitude can be summarized as critical of the United States for having lent its support to the Shah even after it was clear that he was going to be overthrown. One finds an echo of that attitude in an editorial in *Le Monde* of 7/30/80, which followed the death of the Shah.

"Unlike the United States," writes *Le Monde,* "Paris had the ability to take its distance [from the Shah] when it appeared that the future of the regime was extremely precarious. It was the politics of the 'two irons in the fire' in which the activities of Khomeini in Neauphle le Chateau were symbolic. There was extreme satisfaction in France when the Shah fell; France had changed horses at the right time." The editorial goes on to say that by this time France's satisfaction in its policy had declined: "We had reasoned in terms of a change in power; we remain today with an absence of power."

Still, at the time we underook the study of *Le Monde,* it was the period when President Carter and the United States government were putting extreme pressure on its European allies to exercise sanctions against Iran. The foreign ministers of the European Community met in Luxembourg with the Japanese foreign minister on April 21 and 22 to study the U.S. request for sanctions. The request for sanctions, *Le Monde* writes on 4/20/80, "is at the origin of the actual 'transatlantic crisis.' " Perhaps all of *Le Monde*'s views on the relationship between the United States and Europe over the Iran crisis are crystalized in a column written in the newspaper on 4/17/80 by its editor-in-chief André Fontaine, considered by most observers to be the most prestigious journalist of *Le Monde* when it comes to matters of foreign policy.

The points that Fontaine makes appear repeatedly in the columns of *Le Monde.* President Carter is not up to the task. United States power is waning. Europe has its own interests to protect and therefore has nothing to gain in blindly following American policy.

Speaking of a television appearance by President Carter, which had caused *Time* magazine to comment that we have finally seen "some fire in his eyes," Fontaine starts his column, entitled "How to speak strongly with a little stick," by saying:

> Television viewers in France did not have the same impression [as *Time*]. The look of the President of the United States Sunday night made us think of a beaten dog. It wasn't anger, nor even vivacity that emanated from him, but lost innocence, an apologetic softness quite exceptional among those who have bitten once and for all the demon of ambition. It requires a lot of nerve by people as ruthlessly stubborn as Khomeini or as coldly cynical as the Soviets to accuse of blackmail this man visibly not up to the task. One understands that he is wounded and that he has difficulty in admitting that Europe shows so little desire to support him in the face of adversity.

As if that view of Carter were not stern enough, Fontaine continues:

> We cannot hide this fact: The United States and its allies enter this crisis from a position of weakness. The Hamlet-like personality in the White House, his hesitations, his contradictions reflect the state of an empire that has not yet recovered from Vietnam and Watergate, which to stop the rapid fall of the dollar and galloping inflation must resign itself in an election year, which is uncommon, to a good recession, and which finds itself in the field of conventional arms, and even more in manpower, in a situation of clear inferiority to the USSR.

Having established his criteria, Fontaine goes on to make the argument for the reticence of the Europeans to follow the American lead on sanctions:

> What good are sanctions against one of the principal producers of oil in the world? When Iran a year ago cut its production by two million barrels of oil a day, it provoked a doubling of the worldwide price of crude. That can start again, profiting from the trouble that the freeze of Libyan and Algerian exports, notably to the United States, has already provoked. It is true that its [Iran's] economy cannot operate without the sale of energy products, but there is no lack of potential clients in Eastern Europe. And even, if by a miracle, Mr. Carter received from his European allies the solidarity he seeks in an imperative manner, there would always be those who would try to go around it. South Africa has up until now fairly well withstood the economic sanctions imposed against it for its policy of apartheid, and Argentina rushed to furnish the Soviet Union a part of the wheat it was not receiving from the United States because of Afghanistan.

Speaking of the possibility of military intervention in Iran, Fontaine says that the "credibility of Carter's threats is all the more questionable because his gunpowder appears to be soggy from the start. The United States is paying today for the aberration of investing massively in the most sophisticated arms while economizing on manpower." The military effort to liberate the American hostages in Iran took place just nine days after this column was written.

In passing, even a sophisticated observer like Fontaine falls into the mythology about America mentioned in our introduction by describing Ronald Reagan as a "personality from a western movie, next to whom Nixon appears to be a leftist." I have cited this particular column at length, because its theses about the United States appear repeatedly in *Le Monde*.

They come back with insistence in *Le Monde*'s coverage of the failed attempt to free the American hostages. The newspaper's lead editorial of that day, 4/26/80, having underlined the fact that Carter probably would not suffer politically in the United States for having attempted to rescue the hostages, goes on to add:

> Abroad, however, the credibility of the United States will suffer once again. The image of a hesitant and unlucky president will emerge reinforced by an event that will certainly be presented as an analogy of the botched invasion of Cuban exiles at the start of the presidency of Kennedy—as "the poor man's Bay of Pigs." What is there to think about the efficiency of a military apparatus on which depends the security of a good half of the planet, and which is not capable of even landing two planes in a desert before engaging the enemy? What remains of the "Carter Doctrine" that claims to protect Western interests in the entire Gulf region?

Ten days later, in an opinion page consecrated to the subject, "After the American Fiasco," a new thesis appears. Raymond Offroy, a former French ambassador and former member of Parliament, writes that the rescue effort did not succeed because it was not meant to succeed. "What was this affair all about?" Offroy asks. "Evidently to intimidate and impress the Europeans. It was necessary to prove to Paris, Bonn and Rome that the menace of an American military intervention [in Iran], if Atlantic solidarity was not put into total effect, was not an idle threat. It had to prove that if Europe did not engage itself completely in an *American quarrel,* a hazardous initiative that could create an armed conflict was not to be excluded" (emphasis added).

These two themes—the intimidation of Europe and the fact that the taking of the American hostages in Teheran was an "American quarrel"—were not entirely new to the pages of *Le Monde*. At the time of the October War in 1973, the theory that the United States had provoked the conflict between Egypt and Israel and the oil blockade to control its European allies better was a favorite theme of *Le Monde*.

The idea of a Europe feudally attached to the United States is taken up with more ferocity on the same page by Manuel de Dieguez:

> A vacillating president of the United States addresses himself to the populations, heirs of Pericles and the Caesars, passing over the heads of their leaders. Moving a little slowly, Europe gives in on the basic points. The delay, not to say ultimatum, that was assigned to her was respected for almost 24 hours. Does she [Europe] reproach America for its methods? It is not the servitude which causes her pain, but the sad profile of her master. "If you had been strong, how happy we would have been to follow you." Then comes the failure of the military coup. It is too late to dare official surprise over not having been informed.

This last column highlights one of the most evident paradoxes about relationships between Europe and the United States that one can find in the pages of *Le Monde* (and in the higher spheres of European politics as well). There are two theories: either the United States is weak and hesitant, a dangerous state of affairs for the Western alliance; or the United States is constantly scheming and plotting to keep its European allies subservient to American policy. Through the crisis between the United States and Iran, we get these two points of view without anyone's ever commenting on the obvious paradox. Later, however, in dealing with the subject of Afghanistan, we will see that this paradox has not escaped another pillar of *Le Monde,* Michel Tatu.

It must be pointed out in fairness that *Le Monde* published an article on 8/5/80, written by the former Israeli foreign minister Abba Eban, which goes against the theories of most of its writers and contributors. "It is bizarre," Eban writes,

> to see the Europeans ask themselves what "support" Europe should give the United States on the affairs of Afghanistan and Iran. One could think that these are American problems, and that the United States is calling on its indulgent friends to sacrifice for a faraway cause. The truth is that Afghanistan and Iran are at least two times closer to Europe than the United States. Europe would have more trouble than the United States in dealing with a Soviet intrusion in the Gulf oil fields. The integrity of the diplomatic system, injured by the taking of the hostages in Iran, is one of the more remarkable products of European creativity.

The Afghanistan Crisis and the Olympic Games Boycott

Again, it should be noted that our study of *Le Monde* began some months after the intervention of the Soviet Union in Afghanistan. Thus we will not deal here with the first reactions to that invasion, seen in the transatlantic context. Yet, our study started at the time when President Carter and the U.S. government were pushing the Europeans to take a stronger stand against the Soviet invasion, including trying to get the Europeans to boycott the Moscow Olympic Games. It was at the Venice Economic Summit in June that the chief European leaders were to meet President Carter in the context of the American president's demand for a stronger position on Afghanistan. For the first time they recognized both the growing difficulties of the Soviets in Afghanistan and the growing ferocity of the Soviet repression there. In a communiqué the Nine had also acknowledged the "national character" of the Afghan resistance.

It is in this context that we must read the remarkable article of Michel Tatu, who has been *Le Monde*'s correspondent in both Moscow and Washington and is one of the newspaper's most important commentators on foreign affairs. In this article (6/22–23/80), we find the themes expounded by André Fontaine in his article on the Iran crisis, particularly on the disastrous state of the Atlantic alliance. But Tatu, unlike Fontaine, does not lay all these problems at the door of Mr. Carter. Having covered the Carter White House directly in Washington, he has a different evaluation of the president, although he finds it hard to conceal his personal contempt for the man.

Tatu opens his article with a quotation of President Carter in an interview in the Italian daily, *La Stampa*. "The Alliance," Carter is quoted as saying, "is in my opinion stronger than it has been for a number of years, perhaps since it was formed." Tatu attributes this statement to the "rhetorical excesses" of Mr. Carter, statements like his unstinting praise of the Shah of Iran one year before his fall, words that Tatu says should be put down to a man's "having gone beyond his actual thinking."

Carter, Tatu writes, is one of the most talkative presidents in the history of the United States. But having stuck his journalistic lance into the president, he continues:

> That being said, if the state of transatlantic relations on the eve of the Venice meeting is precisely one of the worst seen in 30 years, the fault is not uniquely that of Mr. Carter. The weaknesses of the man who has run the White House for three and a half years are exaggerated, almost with pleasure, as if everything, or almost, came from his "inconsistencies," his "hesitations" and his "ignorance of the world's realities." The reality is that the American president lacks neither intelligence nor character: he knows his dossiers as well as—sometimes even better than—many of his interlocutors. . . . In reality, Mr. Carter has only placed in evidence the decline of the "Imperial Presidency" and crystalized what the Europeans suspected of America under his predecessors, Nixon and Ford: that the power of the executive is paralyzed by Congress; it is a country much more difficult to govern than all the comparable systems in Western Europe, a military

power that is in the process of ceding first place to the USSR. . . . At the same time, the United States has not lost its propensity to "say the truth," to hide behind the moralism of its institutions and its proclaimed goals, to show its allies the path to follow and to act with surprise at the reticence it encounters.

We now come to the center of Tatu's argument, which concerns the relationship between Europe and the United States: "Mr. Carter, having confirmed the American weakness by the failure of his delayed operation at Tabas, was left with no other alternative than to seek from his allies economic and political sanctions against Iran, a more fragile and disputed answer to what was, certainly, a violation of a rights of everyone (rights of diplomats), but also and in the first instance an attack on the prestige of the United States, whose responsibility was therefore principally engaged."

While more subtle, Tatu here again takes up the theme that the taking of the hostages is principally a problem between the United States and Iran: "The allies could not fail to follow, obviously, but their hearts were never in it, as the refusal of the British Parliament to apply the sanctions decided by the Nine clearly shows."

But the heart of Tatu's argument has to do with Afghanistan: "The dissonance that we saw in reaction to the events in Afghanistan is less apparent, but more profound. The Americans can permit themselves to go from détente to tension with the other superpower without great problems; they are *far away*, their relations with the East are relatively recent, and they have never affected daily life in the United States" (emphasis added).

(I pause here to note that as in many cases the action of General de Gaulle is in question here, even if subliminally, for in saying that the United States' relations with the Soviet Union are "recent," Tatu makes oblique reference to the fact that General de Gaulle opened the path toward détente with the Soviet Union.)

"The Europeans, on the other hand," Tatu pursues, "have adopted the habit of placing their security on two elements, if not contradictory, at least distinct—American protection and 'decent ' relations with the USSR."

Without doubt, this last factor varies with distance. Great Britain, a little more isolated from the continent and turned toward the great ocean, has permitted itself and continues to permit itself often to irritate the Kremlin, without worrying too much about the consequences. France—shielded from the armies of the Warsaw Pact by Germany and feeling strong, rightly or wrongly, with its nuclear force—feels just as independent, but feels she must remain attached to détente, preoccupied as she has been since de Gaulle to play a role in the counsels of the great powers and to balance American influence by a "false window" open on Moscow. (There is no suggestion that the founder of the Fifth Republic, who sought balance by supporting the weak, would not in recent years have moved closer to the United States to equalize growing Soviet power; but Gaullism, particularly among those who came to it late, seems to incite more mimicry than capacity for invention.)

In his conclusion, Tatu comes to the problem of the paradoxical reaction to a weak and strong America I mentioned above. Recalling the charges of a condominium launched against the United States at the time of its spectacular rapprochement with the Soviet Union in the early 1970s, Tatu writes: "A good number of those who reproach the brutal conduct of the United States in the times of its splendor, deplore today the absence of leadership in the United States. It is decidedly not possible to be at the same time protected and satisfied."

Those thoughts of Mr. Tatu could have been conveyed to the editorial writer of *Le Monde,* who, in the edition of 5/11–12/80, comments on a speech given by President Carter on foreign policy: "As to Europe, she is once again invited to close ranks and not to believe that her geographic location allows her to play the role of an ostrich in face of Soviet pressures in another part of the world. But if the United States, through the words of its president, has just distributed, sometimes with good reason, blame and lectures of good conduct, it also has not offered any initiatives or creative ideas for leadership, and thus exercises its power more by the 'force of things' than by imagination."

The thoughts of Tatu also apply to a column by André Fontaine on 7/9/80 on the subject of the Soviet intervention in Afghanistan entitled, "A lamb from time to time." Speaking of that intervention, Fontaine says that,

> It is quite possible that at the time of Nixon and Kissinger, the leaders of the Kremlin, impressed by the strength of the United States and by leaders close to them in cynicism and realism, thought of exercising a longstanding condominium, so feared by de Gaulle, Mao, Pompidou and Michel Jobert. Since then, Watergate and the economic crisis that the world struggles against without success probably have made them change their mind. As long as they have the conviction that the "imperialists" have not regained their strength, and it will probably take several years, they will have the tendency to profit from the situation. Others have done like them, starting with the United States itself.

For the French "nouveau philosophe," André Glucksman, the fact that there is a U.S.–USSR condominium is not a matter of doubt. Writing in *Le Monde* of 5/13–14/80 in an article entitled, "The Fear," Glucksman says:

Carter and his American population focus on 50 hostages in a perilous situation but abandon a people in mortal peril (the Afghans). They attempt a rescue operation despite the probability that it will fail, but "forget" to send arms to the guerillas who with naked hands are fighting the strongest infantry in the world. Everything indicates an eventual disgusting barter: I will leave you Afghanistan; I get back my hostages, hands free, if not in Iran, at least in Salvador. This big business ["big business" appears in the article in English] guarantees the two superpowers their private hunting grounds.

As to the call by President Carter for the boycott of the Olympic games, *Le Monde* found itself in the position of arguing the case for traditional French individualism—the right of the athletes to make up their own mind, although it filled its commentary columns with far more articles *for* the boycott than against.

Le Monde's stand was summarized in its editorial of 7/20–21/80, just as the games got under way in Moscow. Saying that one could accord to both partisans and opponents of the boycott "the benefit of sincerity," *Le Monde* writes:

> The motivations of the partisans of the boycott cannot be contested, even in the person of Mr. Carter, whose political motivations were certainly not in evidence in January. To the contrary, the choice does not rest on this subject [politics] but on intimate conviction and "visceral" reaction. The boycott of the Olympic Games could not be a real method of pressure on the Soviet Union because it will be totally without effect in a few days when the games are over. In comparison with the instruments of Realpolitik, which seek a result, the boycott is simply a moral condemnation. More simply still, it translates the legitimate uneasiness that one feels in honoring with one's presence a big celebration in a nation that represses the rights of man and is at this very moment crushing the Afghan people. If there is a real effect [of the boycott], it is because the communist leaders are in permanent search for legitimacy, and wanted to find in these Games a new honorability.

To be noted in the edition of *Le Monde* of the same day is a vehement attack on the boycott written by J. M. Charbonnel, one of the French Olympic team's marathon runners, in which he "refuses to be enrolled in a new manifestation of the ideological confrontation between the blocs."

And *Le Monde*'s correspondent in Moscow, Daniel Vernet, writes on 7/17/80: "It is illusion to think that the proximity of the Olympic Games would have brought about a moderation in Soviet foreign policy or that a concern for the good functioning of the Olympic Games would have pushed the Kremlin to renounce its strategic objective—Afghanistan, specifically. As important as the games are in the life of the USSR, they are not determinant."

The Americans, American Culture, and the English (American) Language

No survey of *Le Monde* and its views of transatlantic relationships would be complete without a study of how it feels about America itself. The editors of *Le Monde* will certainly deny it vehemently, but an American reader is struck by the constant and subtle anti-Americanism that one finds in the pages of *Le Monde*. This is drowned in a flow of laudatory articles about American painting, film, dance, and other arts. But beneath the surface there is the constant view of the Americans as naive children, interested only in money and power, and engaged in a worldwide battle to impose their hegemony on the culture and languages of other countries, notably France.

While *Le Monde* clearly sees the United States as a fading empire—like Rome and Great Britain before it—in political, military, and economic terms, it sees Europe and France losing the cultural struggle with the Anglo-Saxon world, something to be deplored because in their hearts they feel that that world is inferior; they feel it does not have the intellectual roots or tradition that made French culture and language dominant in the world until the latter half of the 19th century.

Mixed with this feeling is the barely concealed dream for a return to the days of French grandeur and power. As Pierre Juillet, a former counselor of President Georges Pompidou, writes in *Le Monde* of 6/11/80: "Today, when the uncertainties and apparent weaknesses of the United States leave the West disoriented and divided, it is France that must again seize the place and role that history has always assigned it, at the head of the free world."

The vision of a naive America turns up in Louis Marcorelles' review of the film, *The Empire Strikes Back*, on 8/23/80. While recognizing that the film may have lost the "formal energy" of its predecessor, *Star Wars*, the reviewer praises the film for its capacity to bring forward an "ethic of common meaning able to mobilize a very large public in the United States," that public consisting of "those adults with the souls of eternal children who through winds and tides wish to believe in happiness at all costs."

Marcorelles goes on to talk about the film's author, George Lucas, whose naivete he calls legendary, claiming that he displays a "profound intuition of the ideological needs of a whole nation" when he announces, like President Carter and Ronald Reagan, the return to strength of an America, "optimistic against all odds."

Perhaps the most edifying example of *Le Monde*'s attitude toward the United States can be found in the July 4, 1980 edition of the newspaper when a page of opinion was consecrated to America's Independence Day. The lead article, written by André Fontaine, and entitled "Where America Triumphs," addresses the reader on two levels. The first is praise of American culture: describing America as "badly governed," "losing its military superiority," "incapable of bringing an end to recession and stagflation," Fontaine goes on to say, "America, which is losing in so many domains, does not cease to win in another—the most important, perhaps: culture."

But no sooner has Fontaine undertaken what appears to be a tribute to America's cultural leadership than he uses the example of the prime vehicle of a culture, its language, to demonstrate what he sees as a kind of American cultural imperialism. Fontaine concedes that English, frequently referred to these days as the "Latin of our times," is currently the "most universal, the most alive and the best adapted language to the needs of the moment."

More in sorrow than in anger, Fontaine points out that French President Valery Giscard d'Estaing uses English to communicate with his friend German Chancellor Helmut Schmidt and with Soviet Foreign Minister Andrei Gromyko. He goes on to say: "Every day there are seminars in France, where English is spoken. . . . It is impossible to exercise certain trades without speaking English. . . . A study by the University of Orsay makes the point that of 615 articles recently published by 185 French professors and researchers, only 142, or 23 percent, were in our language." And Fontaine asks himself: "Would it not be wiser to resign ourselves to the inevitable and only speak English, and to reserve to a minority of erudites, the study of languages condemned like French, German, Russian, Spanish, or Arabic, as if the principal crime in the history of a people will have been to stay too small in a world becoming too big? There are people who will say that. Others, even more numerous, think it and resign themselves unconsciously."

Fontaine explains that it is the fact that American English is not tied to a particular national culture that allows it to project itself into space and the future, rather than being constricted by the need to preserve its traditions. And for Fontaine, language is but one cultural vehicle. He points out that the American cultural model goes way beyond the limits of language. He notes that in Stalin's day, Coca Cola was seen as the very symbol of American imperialism. Today it is produced in every country of the Eastern bloc.

Fontaine fears that this proliferation of the American language and cultural symbols risks the demise of what he refers to as the "fabulous kaleidoscope of universal culture." Interestingly, though, he sees a ray of hope for salvation in the current wave of regional nationalism, citing the reawakening of Islam as a prime example.

On the same page, as a counterpoint to Fontaine's article, a devastating attack on American culture deems it totally worthless. Written by Jean Claude Barreau, who is the director of a French publishing house, it is entitled, "A country that does not work well." Charging that the French government only wants to make France "an America on the Seine," Barreau goes on to say that with the exception of a "few successes always cited as examples," like the "power of the press," "the beauty of its musical rhythms," and some films, one can "see the bad functioning of American society in a number of fields."

An example: "The level of culture of the people of the Middle West is incredibly low, even in cities as populated as Lyon. It would be impossible, for example, to find in a country with four times the population of our own, a million people to read a newspaper of the quality of *Le Monde.*" Mr. Barreau has apparently never heard of *The New York Times.*

Other examples: "Violence in American society is almost without equivalent. Paris, at night, is a paradise compared to New York." "Politics: in the words of Jacques Thibau, they have perfected 'the most insidious system of colonialism which has ever existed.' " "Scientific: American research would not work so well without the immense, worldwide brain 'racket,' brains purchased by piles of dollars." To conclude, Barreau writes: "That state is basically devouring. It has developed like a cancer on the world."

This is all, of course, quite excessive and there are probably many editors of *Le Monde* who would disagree with Mr. Barreau. But what a strange choice of article to select for an apparently objective attempt to look at America on the Fourth of July!

I could go on at length on this subject, but I believe the examples above suffice to make my point.

The Middle East

During the months treated by our study, there were two noticeable periods of active discussion in *Le Monde* about the Middle East conflict. The first was in early to mid-June, both preceding and following the announcement of a Common Market initiative in the area, as distinct from the Camp David negotiations. In the first days of June, despite the announcement of the European Nine, then already dating back several weeks, of their intention to take an initiative in the Middle East, *Le Monde* saw the likelihood of their encountering what Philippe Lemaitre on 6/4/80 described as the United States' immediate and vigorous proclamation of "their hostility toward a project that they consider to be untimely meddling." The most that could be expected from the Venice Common Market Meeting of June 12 and 13, then, when the subject was to be broached, was, Lemaitre predicted, "the publication of a moderate declaration by which the Nine, worried all the same, to make a sign in the direction of the Arabs, could declare themselves in favor of a Palestinian state." This would be to the center of the French position on the subject.

In its editorial of 6/15/80, following the Venice meeting, Le Monde voices its surprise in describing the Common Market declaration on the Middle East to be "of a better quality than one could have feared." While the declaration "certainly doesn't constitute a great step forward as compared with the French position," Le Monde asks, "Is this necessarily a bad thing?" Once the Nine had decided to exchange their points of view, why, Le Monde asks, would they have aligned themselves with the most advanced theses, in other words, those of Paris? Isn't it important that after much trial and error, and laborious dealings, they had succeeded in coming to agreement on a common main idea?

Posing the question whether it is in fact a new idea (of course not, France thought of it ages ago), Le Monde cites the key notion of the Venice declaration as being the simultaneous achievement of the Palestinians' recognition of Israel's right to exist in guaranteed and secure borders and the recognition by Israel of the Palestinians' right to self-determination. But, Le Monde stresses, such a task is immense and implies a very strong political will. Are the European leaders really motivated by such a determination, or are they only trying to distance themselves from Washington, which is paralyzed by the presidential campaign, and from Jerusalem, which is increasingly closing itself off in a policy of obstinacy, not to say provocation?

The only thing to do, in Le Monde's view, is wait and see what initiative the president of the EEC takes, once the EEC sees whether the United States modifies its stand before the United Nations Security Council following the American presidential elections and the "failure" of the Camp David negotiations. For, Le Monde is convinced, "It is clear that any initiative, in order to materialize, will need a certain American support, if only for the reason that only the U.S. has, if any country does, the means to convince Israel."

In any case, Le Monde observed that the EEC declaration came at a time of great turbulence within the EEC itself, thus weakening its impact and believability. The "failure" of the Camp David negotiations, however, along with a possible shift of the American position might come sooner than expected, Le Monde speculated, and it would be more and more up to Europe to show its true colors on this issue.

The second period of Le Monde's special treatment of the Middle East situation started in late July, following the Israel Knesset's adoption of a law on July 23 that annexed East Jerusalem onto Israel. At that time, *Le Monde's* editorial of 7/25/80 pointed out, "Mr. Begin intends to move the prime minister's office to the Arab part of the city. This gesture is provocative not only for the Arab population, but for all the friends of Israel." Even the United States, *Le Monde* observes, refuses, like most countries, to establish its embassy in Jerusalem and will not visit the head of government at that location. This is the time for Europe to act in order to avoid the further worsening of the Arab-Israeli conflict. The 7/25/80 editorial concludes by saying, "It remains that other steps, like that taken by the Europeans in favor of the new approach by the parties concerned in the conflict, including the PLO, will appear increasingly necessary if one is to put an end to this dangerous disintegration."

The American abstention from the August 20 adoption of a United Nations Security Council resolution condemning the East Jerusalem annexation did nothing in *Le Monde's* view to appease the Arab leaders. *Le Monde* cites in its 8/22/80 editorial the call for a holy war voiced by Saudi Arabia in mid-August despite that country's being a faithful ally of the United States. The editorial goes on to say that "despite the good will of its president," Egypt has found it "necessary to interrupt the negotiations at Camp David" and to "delay further negotiations on Palestinian autonomy until after the American presidential elections." After all, *Le Monde* points out, Begin has "nothing to lose, at least in appearance. He knows very well that President Carter won't desert him only a few weeks before the presidential elections."

The underlying assumption was that once the U.S. elections were over, the United States would modify its Mideast tactics, which would then come closer to the European, if not specifically the French, line of thought in the subject. (In this case the ideal of the lone horseman fails—in favor, perhaps, of having trained the stampede!)

World Economic Picture

The months covered by this study were marked by a period of political crisis that tended to obscure media coverage of the world economic crisis, and *Le Monde* was no exception to this. *Le Monde*, however, ran several analyses of the world economic picture within the framework of European-American relations. Ultimately, America's loss of ground on the economic front became yet another political argument for the end of undisputed American leadership and in favor of a new international economic order in which Europe and specifically France would play a leading role.

On the front page of the 8/29/80 edition of *Le Monde*, Jean Pierre Chevenement, a deputy of the Socialist Party and a frequent contributor to the paper, argues that while international monetary questions may well be disguised as "theses," they are first and foremost political questions. He sees it as the role of the French Socialist Party to denounce what he calls "the deficiencies and complacencies of Giscard and Barre, draped in a hypocritical orthodoxy, and to explain to the French the decisive political stakes of international monetary problems."

From the aftermath of World War II, when American dollars rebuilt a war-torn Europe, through the pumped-up American economy of the Vietnam War years, the Yankee dollar was unquestionably the driving force of the world economy. Not so any more, *Le Monde* pointed out at every opportunity, faithfully chronicling the fall of the U.S. dollar on the world market. European currencies were, for the time being, the stronger ones. Internally, America was marked by stagflation, a continuing high rate of unemployment, and suffering as much as anyone from the impact of the second oil price shock. In spite of all these self-evident truths, *Le Monde* charged that the United States continued to act in a protectionist manner, in its own interests, still basking in an economic heyday that had long since gone down the drain.

Chevenement claims that the current "disorder" of the international monetary system benefits certain countries, in the first place the United States, which "has renounced all discipline, but none of its privileges." This is, according to Chevenement, actually an "organized disorder" that "serves the interests of the 'American Empire.' "

A *Le Monde* editorial of 6/22/80, following the Venice summit meeting, entitled "Skepticism," points out that experience has shown that anti-protectionist agreements have not prevented national interests from coming first, but the only example given is that of the United States.

The United States, "rich among the rich" for so many years, has become accustomed to an ever-increasing bounty, and it is not to be expected that it will relinquish it too quickly, *Le Monde* warns. In reference to the Soviet grain embargo, Michel Cicurel, in an article on 4/18/80 called, "A too easy world," says that "it is more difficult to deprive the Americans of luxuries than the Soviets of essentials," and illustrates this by pointing out that the contracts for provisions of grain to the Soviet Union were immediately bought by the American government. This, for Cicurel, demonstrates that the Carter administration "displays spontaneously and publicly its convictions that the American people are unwilling to undergo the hardships of an economic war."

Le Monde's attitude regarding Carter's economic plan was that it was engineered as a vote-getting strategy, particularly for American blacks who bitterly reproached him for not following through in his promises of the previous election. In any case, New York correspondent Nicole Bernheim says on 8/30/80 that "politics probably plays a more important role than the recession in Carter's proposal for the creation of a million more jobs before 1982."

The answer to a world economy marked by outmoded American self-interest is, in the view of *Le Monde,* a new brand of multipolar economy. Chevenement argues (8/29/80) that "the reform of the monetary system with France playing a special role cannot be dissociated from a new relationship of forces and a new organization of international society. The days of unshared hegemony of the United States are over," says Chevenement, even if the United States is, he admits, still by far the principal world power. This criticism of so-called American hegemony is an institution in *Le Monde,* going back to the early days of Beauve-Mery.

Chevenement goes on to say that it is "only in developing a powerful and diversified industry, in containing the pressure of imports, in launching a fight against the profound causes of inflation and in building its independence in the area of energy that France will escape its too encumbering protectors and too pushy advisors."

While arguing for a multipolar economic system, *Le Monde* is hardly less critical of its Common Market allies than it is of the United States. Danger is seen in the German effort to win energy sources from the Middle East and take unfair advantage of African natural resources. The United Kingdom, in the aftermath of the Lamb War and the fisherman's blockade, is viewed as trailing on America's coat tails in an effort to reestablish a joint hegemony. Not only is the dollar not to be trusted, but in a sequel (8/30/80) to his above-mentioned article, Chevenement says that only a return to a gold-based international market will truly transform the current monetary system. He argues that "it must be remembered that the good functioning of the European monetary system during the past year is essentially due to the weakness—however temporary—of the German balance of payments."

The Brandt Commission Report on aid to the Third World is seen by *Le Monde* as being an unrealistic utopian dream. It is again and again pointed out that despite all the international meetings held each year at the United Nations, the OECD, and elsewhere for the purpose of helping the Third World, protectionism—particularly the American brand—increases, and aid to the developing world declines.

In the 6/17/80 edition, Francisco Vergara poses the question: "As for the United States and Japan, why would they favor an industrial expansion that would facilitate the modernization of the industrial apparatus of their competitor, Old Europe?" Vergara goes on to say that the reasoning of the Brandt Commission is based on the "tacit hypothesis that the North (in the North-South dialogue) constitutes a united whole," while really it "is nothing more than an abstract being." The North, says Vergara, "as it exists in reality, doesn't seem to have a common interest in the development of the Third World." Besides, he asks, does it have a common interest in anything?

But France, it is argued, *does* have an interest in supporting the Third World, and Third Worldism is, in fact, one of *Le Monde*'s traditional pet causes. Chevenement not only points out (8/30/80) that it is in the interest of France to distance itself from the American economic leadership which has lost its clout, but resorts to Gaullic paternalism in saying that it is the vocation of France to combine its ambition with that of the great human cause. He emphasizes France's historical ties with the Third World and the USSR to forward his opinion that France may play a leading role in a new economic order. *Le Monde* is quick to point out that what they consider to be one of the positive proposals of the Brandt Commission—the bringing of public aid to the Third World to 0.7 percent of GNP—is rejected by the United States while it is a goal to be reached by France by 1985.

Response to Salinger

France First

Recalling Henri Pierre's criticism of *The Times* (London) for vacillating in its choice between Carter and Reagan, Pierre Salinger said, "*Le Monde* didn't make up its mind about the U.S. election either." Its coverage, he said, was "workmanlike and even-handed" but given to caricature—"It was Mr. Peanuts versus Mr. Cowboy." Upon Reagan's victory, *Le Monde* expressed the fear that the new president held "a simplistic conception of the U.S.–European dialogue." That judgment, Salinger observed, showed how self-contradictory *Le Monde* could be. "For years, it deplored a lack of leadership in the U.S.; now it worries about an 'American monologue.' "

Le Monde often uses examples drawn from the United States, added Salinger, "to chide the government or people in France on comparable issues." A five-part series on the costs and compromises of political campaign financing in the United States helped "to shed a cold light, disconcerting to Frenchmen, on practices in France."

Le Monde enjoys, in Salinger's words, "an absolutely capital position in French society—it's a newspaper you *must* read. . . . To read the stories from their correspondents in Warsaw or Teheran is to feel you're living there." *Le Monde* is the only Paris daily that makes money and has improved its circulation in recent years, despite its being "a very serious newspaper of record." It wields influence with the government, but in recent years less as a spokesman for government policy than as a voice of opposition, quite critical at times. (A few days before Salinger made that comment, the Minister of Justice, citing several *Le Monde* articles that appeared over a period of months, moved to indict its top editors on a criminal charge of bringing disrepute upon the administration of French justice.)

Henri Pierre argued that, by his citations, Salinger himself had demonstrated that *Le Monde* does not follow just one line, but expresses a range of views. Pierre did admit to *Le Monde*'s general adherence to a Gaullist line, but added, "Everyone in France has been a Gaullist—unfortunately, not at the same time."

Le Monde's editorial stance toward the United States, said Jan Reifenberg, betrays an ambivalence: "Condescension and criticism are mixed with the hope that the U.S. will maintain its strength in Europe and the world."

William Pfaff, a writer who lives in Paris, explained *Le Monde*'s attitude toward France's allies in this way: "It's not *Le Monde* alone, but France itself that feels—perhaps the last country to do so—that it is in moral competition with the rest of the world."

Renaud Vignal, a French government press officer, suggested it would be wrong to make too much of any apparent anti-German sentiment in *Le Monde*: "It merely reflects France's sense of economic inferiority next to Germany's dominance in this respect."

Melvin Lasky of *Encounter* argued, however, that the pattern of anti-American and anti-German feelings expressed in *Le Monde* was persistent in a way that could not be explained by economic rivalry alone. It would be typical of *Le Monde*, he said—on learning that Germany, out of sensitivity to the past, was issuing its soldiers not jackboots, but gum-soled shoes—to say, " 'Gumsoles, eh? Next time we won't even hear them coming.' " With *Le Monde*, it is "not so much a matter of uncertainty as to what kind of leadership they want in the U.S. or Germany—whatever it is will be wrong." The major tendencies in the United States, Britain, and Germany toward transatlantic cooperation and tolerance, Lasky said, are not present in France, "where deference is demanded as the first condition of cooperation."

A tone of superiority in matters dealing with the United States or Germany—"a tone that runs from flip to snide"—was something that Mort Rosenblum also found in *Le Monde*. But it is balanced, he said, by the way *Le Monde*'s writers so skillfully describe the "feel" of a situation.

Reporting on Germany

Peter Galliner of the International Press Institute said he was not surprised to hear *Le Monde* attacked for being anti-German. He questioned, however, whether this charge was deserved so much as it reflected the fact that any criticism of the German government, whether in print or on television, "leads to an outburst in the Federal Republic." Many foreign correspondents in Bonn, he maintained, have consequently made a habit of sending out stories that contain not a word of criticism. The reflex reactions in Germany to any critical press are mostly unjustified in Galliner's view: "In other countries, such irritating stories would be sloughed off."

Peter Corterier, a member of the German Bundestag, granted that German officials might be too sensitive to criticism, but said that while he felt that *Le Monde* was otherwise one of the best papers, its past coverage of terrorism in Germany was "truly terrible—it actually helped to spread terrorist propaganda, and it went on for months."

To believe that is an overreaction, claimed Galliner. That *Le Monde* might be critical, he said, did not justify charges that it is anti-German. The larger point is that "it's getting harder and harder for journalists to report responsibly on the German scene." He cited the complaint of a Bonn correspondent that it was difficult for foreign journalists in Germany to arrange interviews, even group interviews, with Chancellor Schmidt.

To that, a Bonn press official replied that to his knowledge Schmidt gave more interviews to foreign correspondents than any other head of government in the West. He denied any attempt to constrain correspondents in Bonn, but admitted, "We do object to clichés when they appear, and we worry about so many cheap films that portray Germans as stupid, jackbooted villains."

Niels Hansen of the Foreign Office in Bonn said he was taken aback by Galliner's description of the pressures on foreign correspondents in Germany. "Our explosive outbursts have been rare," he said. "We're comparatively lenient in our view of the press, perhaps the least nationalistic in what we expect." But for him, too, foreign television programs like *Hogan's Heroes* were a source of genuine grievance.

Galliner thought it "typical" that both officials should cite fictional television programs and films to support their concern, rather than to notice the many positive things reported about Germany in the postwar period.

Jonathan Carr of the London *Financial Times* told of his own experience as a foreign correspondent in Bonn. Of all the capitals, Bonn provides the easiest access to information, he said. "Getting answers to your questions is not difficult there." One does react, he granted, to the danger of falling into clichés, so that, if anything, "one may err by giving an overly friendly view of the Federal Republic—even Vinocur [of *The New York Times*] seems to be shifting in this direction." In any case, Carr said, an observer has to conclude that Germany today is "a well-run democratic country—it's the foreign diplomats in Bonn, not government officials, who keep saying this." An interview with Schmidt, on the other hand, "is not an unmixed blessing. It can be revealing but unpleasant."

Jan Reifenberg confirmed that Chancellor Schmidt "was not enamoured with the press, and he tends to teach, to impose, and not to suffer fools gladly." Reifenberg also granted Galliner's point that Germans may be too sensitive to criticism. "It's an historical thing. It stems from the earnest attempt in the postwar years to convey a new image." At the same time, he was glad to support Carr's judgment of Bonn's openness to corre-spondents. Rating their cooperativeness with the press, he said, he would give Bonn an "A," London a "B" or "C," but Paris an "E."

William Pfaff suggested that both overreactions and bias arise from a "sense of vulnerability." Whatever might have been true before, "France today," he said, "is entirely relaxed about Germany—because the French no longer have reason to feel inferior."

The Bonn press official agreed that foreign reporting of Germany had become more balanced over the years. The exception, he said, was the new cliché to appear in the American press, namely, that Germany seemed to be headed toward neutrality, toward "Finlandization," a charge he denied.

Tomorrow's Journalists

The journalists of *Le Monde*'s early years generally tried—and tended—to be objective, according to Henri Pierre, but today's younger new people are politically committed: "They express their personal opinions every day on every detail. As a consequence, we are losing our authority with readers."

It was *Le Monde*'s staff, Pierre pointed out, who elected Claude Julien to be the new editor—a choice that did not sit well with *Le Monde*'s share-holders who were concerned about what Salinger called Julien's "basically anti-American" line in his previous position as head of the foreign affairs section.

Renaud Vignal did not think there was any leftist plot to take control of *Le Monde*. Rather, he felt, the new journalists simply reflect the young, edu-cated people of France today. Vignal emphasized that *Le Monde* was the only French newspaper whose control is shared with its journalists, not held exclusively by its private owners. The government, he said, consid-ered it the most reliable outlet for making French foreign policy clear, but also the most critical. He cited *Le Monde*'s attack on President Giscard d'Estaing for venturing to Warsaw, more or less in disregard of the allies, for a personal meeting with Leonid Brezhnev at a time when the United States and others were still trying to isolate the Soviet Union because of its invasion of Afghanistan.

Mort Rosenblum, from his perspective at the *International Herald Tribune*, questioned *Le Monde*'s approach to facts, its failure to insist on hard report-ing. "It's getting worse and more politicized," he said, "and, yes, especially with the younger reporters." He granted, "It's so much easier to sit back somewhere, look at the larger picture, get off rather good phrases and do the color—and *not* get out and follow down a story." To illustrate this, he cited an article, though he was "not 100 percent sure it was in *Le Monde*— but if it wasn't, it ought to have been."

"There was a long, learned article, just after Pol Pot got going, about the power struggle in Cambodia between two leaders—who had the upper swing, who was more likely to influence foreign policy, and what not. This was great, except that it turned out later that they were both the same person! They were both Pol Pot! He just had a long name, and the writer had taken the first half of the name to talk about one guy and the second half to talk about the other and didn't realize it."

Charles Douglas-Home of *The Times* (London) commented that in Britain, too, the new recruits to journalism all seemed linked to "gauchist values." He explained, "Those are the ones who come forward." This tendency was aggravated in Britain, he said, by agreements with unions that no one could be added to a London staff who had not already had at least three years experience in the provinces. That further narrowed an editor's choice of new people.

Günther Gillessen of the *Frankfurter Allgemeine Zeitung* said that the relationship of leftists to others among journalists on German radio stations was four to one, but Friedhelm Kemna of *Die Welt* took exception. He said that, politically, most candidates for journalistic careers in Germany now were right down the center—"a swing back from the trend of the '60s."

Eugene Blabey of United Press International said that the United States, in contrast to Europe, offered the editor a "buyer's market" in journalists. "You can be discriminating in whom you hire, and they're anxious to please—except they're not anxious to take foreign assignments." (Getting U.S. journalists to go overseas is not a problem for *television* news organizations, declared Pierre Salinger, admitting that greater income, perquisites, and visibility might explain the difference.)

The big contrast between Europe and the United States in recruiting news professionals, according to the *Los Angeles Times'* Brussels correspondent, Murray Seeger, is that "we train people especially for journalism and so these students are not so politicized."

Douglas-Home, on reflection, said it might be an error to attribute "a leftist tendency as such" to young journalists. Rather, they display "the trait of dismissive—or even destructive—criticism."

Reifenberg echoed that view but seemed untroubled by it: "The younger generation in Germany is more critical, not necessarily leftist. Editors and politicians must not dress them down for this, but instead incorporate them into the working process. Be relaxed: let them come along."

Tributes

"If there weren't *Le Monde*," said Mort Rosenblum, "everybody could not survive—it would be like no croissants in France." But to get the benefit of it, you must, he advised, more than with most newspapers, "watch who's writing, what his politics are, and take those into account."

"*Le Monde*'s triumph," stated Charles Douglas-Home, "is that it vindicates, in the journalistic sense, the belief that to connect with a supporting readership, you don't have to do big pictures or otherwise strive to be popular." He asked, perhaps with the difficulties of *The Times* in mind, whether this success was necessarily unique to France. "*Le Monde* doesn't mind arriving with the news a day late. It doesn't mind sleeping on a story so it has time to get it right." All the British press has become homogenous by having to go to press at the same time, while *Le Monde* among French newspapers, because it comes out in the afternoon, "can luxuriate in its few extra hours."

All the suspicion of *Le Monde*'s being anti-American, anti-German, or anti-British, Pierre Salinger concluded, can be explained by the fact that it was Charles de Gaulle who founded it. De Gaulle was a nationalist, and what he stood for remains *Le Monde*'s point of reference. This newspaper lives as "de Gaulle's only legitimate heir."

—MR

INDEX

ABOUT THE AUTHORS

Jonathan Carr has been Bonn correspondent of the London *Financial Times* since 1977. His other foreign postings have included Geneva, Paris, Brussels, and Munich. A journalist since 1964, he was educated—in economics—at Brighton College, Sussex, and Pembroke College, Cambridge.

Henri Pierre was born into a journalistic tradition. His father was managing editor of *Le Temps,* the predecessor of *Le Monde,* where Pierre himself started work in December 1944. After seven years as assistant to the Foreign Editor, he was posted to Washington, then London, Moscow, back to London, Washington again, and now London again—a career as a *Le Monde* foreign correspondent that extends to nearly three decades. His academic degrees were earned at the Université de Paris and the Ecole des Sciences Politiques.

Jan G. Reifenberg has served as the *Frankfurter Allgemeine Zeitung*'s political correspondent in Washington—except for the period from 1965 to 1972 when he was posted in Paris—since 1955. Of his more than 30 years as a journalist, he has spent 20 in on-the-scene coverage of U.S. national politics. Born in Frankfurt, he studied at various universities, receiving the D.Sc. degree from the University of Freiburg/Brsg. His writings include the book, *Notiert in Washington, 1955–63—von Eisenhower bis Kennedy,* published in 1963.

Michael Rice, as a Senior Fellow of the Aspen Institute, conducts inquiries and conferences in the area of communications and media issues. Besides this book, his projects involving journalism have dealt with the role of the news media in the governance of democratic societies, Hispanic-Americans and the mass media in the United States, and the practice and influence of U.S. television news. From 1965 to 1978, he was with WGBH, the public television and radio station in Boston, where such series as *The Advocates, Nova, Arabs and Israelis, World, The Real America,* plus others in the arts and for children, were developed and produced under his management for national broadcast. He was educated at Harvard and as a Rhodes Scholar at Oxford.

Pierre Salinger is the Paris correspondent and bureau chief for ABC News, a division of the American Broadcasting Company, one of the United States' three national commercial television broadcast networks. He was Press Secretary to Presidents Kennedy and Johnson, served briefly as Senator from California in 1964, and, among his business positions, was Vice-President for International Affairs for Continental Airlines, Inc. The author of four books, he has also written for various American and French periodicals.